THE BRIDGE

OVER

THE RIVER

THE BRIDGE
OVER
THE RIVER

Translated from the German
by
JOSEPH WETZL

ANTHROPOSOPHIC PRESS

Copyright © 1974
by The Anthroposophic Press, Inc.

Library of Congress Card No. 74–83229
ISBN 910142–59–9

10 9 8 7 6 5 4 3

Printed in the United States of America.

INTRODUCTION

This volume contains direct communications from a so-called dead individual. Many such messages from the world beyond have been published in recent years, but they have been obtained via mediums in seances, through self-imposed trance, by automatic writing or typing, or through hypnosis.

How do the communications in this volume differ? This will become evident in the following lines, and also in the messages themselves.

As the subtitle indicates, these are "Communications from the life after death of a young artist who died in World War One." Sigwart, a promising musician, was born in Munich, Germany, in 1884. Even in his earliest youth he showed a strong musical talent, and at the age of eight he composed songs that he accompanied himself, as well as little pieces for the piano. Later, he studied music and, besides other musical works, composed an opera that was performed with great success half a year after his death.

At the beginning of the war he enlisted in the army as a volunteer with the fire of enthusiasm with which, at that time the youth of all Europe could still be aroused. After Sigwart's boot training in the cavalry, he had to spend idle time in the rear of the Western Front to his great disappointment. Half a year later he managed to be transferred to the Russian front where, during an attack in

Galicia on May 9th, 1915, he suffered a bullet wound in the lungs and succumbed on June 2nd, 1915.

Sigwart was intimately connected with one of his sisters during his lifetime, and it was with her that he tried to communicate immediately after his death. Finally, after almost two months striving, he was able to convince her of his identity. The sister experienced her brother's initial attempts to reach her in the form of an inner unrest, which eventually culminated in the strong feeling that her brother Sigwart expected something of her, but she could not bear the thought of associating his memory with mediumistic or spiritistic practices. After some time, however, an inner awakening enabled her to establish contact with her brother in full consciousness.

She described the experience thus to another sister: "In the seclusion and quietness of these past days I have come to recognize what Sigwart expects of me, which is not to guide my hand and influence it externally; rather, I myself must open a door in my mind; then I shall hear the words I have to write down."

The difference between this kind of communication and those of mediums cannot be emphasized forcefully enough. This was confirmed by a message from Sigwart himself on July 28, 1916, almost a year later, which read in part: "You know well that my kind of communication can never be as perfect as a message written verbatim on paper via a medium. My kind of transmission, however, is far more sublime than that of automatic writing. For the latter any average medium has the ability, whereas here a certain degree of spiritual development is necessary, or else it would be impossible."

In order to erase any doubts as to the validity of the messages, his sister decided in November, 1915 to submit the by now voluminous papers to Rudolf Steiner, the modern initiate and seer, the creator of Anthroposophy who kept them for several weeks. It will suffice to mention here that Dr. Steiner, who died in 1925, left a legacy of fundamental books and more than 6000 lectures on his spiritual investigations as a *conscious* clairvoyant. There he describes in detail life after death and reincarnation.

The sister describes her subsequent meeting with Dr. Steiner in her own words thus, "For an hour and three quarters he scrutinized page after page in my presence; he cast light on some, for me, incomprehensible passages, explained what Sigwart meant by them, and asked me questions. Many times Rudolf Steiner nodded and exclaimed approvingly, 'Very well described! Well expressed! Characterized exactly! Yes, those musical performances, they are realities!' I waited in vain for the negation of any of the messages; none came! As a parting word Dr. Steiner said, 'Yes, these are exceptionally clear, absolutely authentic communications from the spiritual world. I see no reason for dissuading you from listening to them further.' He added that transmissions of *this* kind are very rare. I felt that Dr. Steiner experienced real joy, and was glad with us and for us."   It naturally became a question as to whether it was advisable to publish these intimate messages. After years of deliberation, all the personalities concerned with the German edition of them felt that the times and conditions of our era demanded that these communications be made known. But in the epilogue of the original German volume the sentiment is expressed that "one would like to surround these pages, which harbor seeds of light, with a protecting mantle to prevent them from becoming the victims of the corroding acid of the cynical and cold intellect."

Above and beyond these considerations came the call from the spiritual world itself, "The time is at hand!"

Sigwart's Masters permitted him to report that "The time has come when we have allowed our Brother to let God's gift be known to wider circles. What he has been permitted to convey to you should now be disseminated in order to bestow blessings, to heal sorrow, to exalt humanity, and to point the way to the light. THE TIME IS AT HAND!" (April 25, 1932.)

In the course of these messages it soon becomes apparent that the identity "Sigwart" had attained an enhanced consciousness in a relatively short time that enabled him to gain important insight into the world beyond. He advances quickly to the astral plane and further into the devachanic spheres. In contrast, it may be noted that the communications one reads of the mediumistic type stem almost exclusively from souls who are still earth-bound, "just beyond the thin veil" that separates them from those of us living on earth.

JOSEPH WETZL

Easter 1973
Spring Valley, N.Y.

PREFACE

The subsequent messages of a young artist who died in the first world war appeared first in the form of a transcript published privately in limited numbers at Whitsuntide 1950. The person who received those messages and wrote them down introduced them with the following preface:

Sigwart!—We had shelted his legacy for many years, anxiously concerned that harsh thoughtlessness through ignorance might not disturb the threads that connected us with him, our brother. Now, as many arms are reaching for his worlds in these bitter times of distress, his words shall also sound to others for consolation and hope.

We also believed then that we could never be happy again since he and his comprehensive musical creativity were torn from us by the war. Too deep was the breach in our innermost communion. Yet his strong power of soul and our love tempered in sorrow overcame the separating grief. From cosmic distances, across time and space, his words sounded timidly at first, then more distinctly, first in the heart of the sister who had been closest to him in life. He called on the souls who could receive his words in lucidity of spirit and in wakeful consciousness.

Thus we partook in his life of spirit. His love built the bridge of light across which we met him joyfully. May his words resound also within other souls and give them the certainty that an intimate bond connects us with the departed ones and their world. Whoever seeks in humility and bows in reverence may also hear in time the faint call that sounds to him in love from the beyond.

M. and L.

Whitsuntide 1950

THE BRIDGE
OVER
THE RIVER

I myself speak, I, your brother Sigwart, who loves you, who is around you and is ardently interwoven with all of you.

You should not mourn anymore, this is so agonizing for me. You must free yourselves from the thought of pain. You were always my sisters and brothers, and so shall it always be.—I see, you have comprehended and accepted everything correctly; now nothing can separate us anymore. Tell the other brothers and sisters and our parents, whom I thank for everything.

You must become the mediator; I have accomplished this contact after long struggles. I willed it from the very beginning, but you did not react.

I am coming steadily nearer to you through your love and understanding. You will all be happy because through me you shall advance and be able to learn much, for I died for you also, in order to transmit the teachings of the spirit to you.

I am satisfied with all of you now. Your grief tormented me in the beginning for I had made the greatest effort to make myself susceptible to you. It is better now.

How easy dying is! I am not permitted to tell you everything, but it goes very, very well with me; you must think of me as a shape formed of light, who need not endure suffering any longer.

I have brought about my own death because here I have greater works to do. You can form no conceptions of these tasks; you cannot divine even how beautiful, how great, how perfect these are.

Hail him, who may fulfill them!

Your body wants rest. Sleep as much as you can. We come together in sleep and help each other. Soon you will also be aware in the waking state.—This is the very beginning.

If you only knew the beauty I have already experienced here! But I shall show all this to you in time to come.

Inevitable laws are about you, which force you to live your life as you have determined it yourself. Divine powers guide it all, but you are shaping your own destiny.

July 30, 1915

You should not doubt anymore. I have to tell you so much more,—why do you not firmly believe in me, in my nearness?—I shall not be permitted to stay connected with you for long in this way, therefore take advantage of it as long as I, your brother Sigwart, speaks through you.

Think not that now, as your brother in the spirit, I am less able to share in your joys than as a human being. I have not changed, except I bear no physical body; I know much more now, and I am happy to be allowed to fulfill a great mission. Otherwise I have stayed the same as you knew me.—Surely, now you doubt no more.

And now something more of the "other world" as you call it. Everything is so much more pure and clear. I did not think I would see it as such in so short a time. Thanks to my interests in supersensible teachings I have experienced no disappointments. To the contrary, death was an awakening more beautiful than I could have imagined.

4

Everything intruded upon me, and I was conscious at once of what had happened to me, that is, that I had stepped through the portals of death, as you so rightly call it.

I had suffered much toward the end of my life on earth.—The shedding of matter proceeds in a condition of sleep; consciousness returns gradually, and then the enjoyment of freedom begins, if one has not been a novice in these things.—

How comforting it is not to have a physical body anymore!—But then the longing returns for the loved ones whom one has left behind. One perceives their grief, and that is terrible!—These were the only real agonies for me, and they still are to a certain extent. But now you know how I am, and you have no more reason to mourn.

Such a moment of pain came to me again just now. You are looking at my picture and you think I am still alive because you see me bodily before you,—suddenly you become conscious of the reality, and then pain stirs it all up again.—These are always backward steps for you.

No separation exists for those who are connected by the bonds of love, which never ceases, not through life, not through death!—

July 31, 1915

The mental images you are forming of me are not correct. I have not as yet disposed fully of the sheaths of the material world, therefore the ease of communication with you. It will be different later, more beautiful and more spiritualized, because I shall continue to shed more of the material substances. For this reason I may not approach you then as easily as now, but you must not think I shall

5

be gone completely. I am living with you through the bond of love, which is more intensive than during lifetime, because now I can be *within* you. Therefore the intimate contact. But I shall not be able to make myself as susceptible to you as now, where no—absolutely no obstacles are between us.

Could you only perceive the appearance of everything here! A world the more real, the more true than yours because in yours all is mere semblance, and people do not see each other as they really are. No one can pretend here because one sees through the beings.

All this is great and sublime as soon as one stands above it. I can survey much now but not everything by far. The new surroundings influence me so strongly that it leaves me frequently unclear as to how much my spirit is able to penetrate it all. (Minor disturbance.)

. . . You must believe in your power, otherwise these communications will be impossible on account of the strong influences surrounding you. You must distinguish correctly as soon as something strange intervenes.—Almost no hindrances would exist for me if you would try to be more courageous.

August 2, 1915

I know more, I can see farther than before, but one is not instantaneously omniscient after having disposed of the material body! A great power lies within every human being, but how few recognize it.—I myself comprehend only now how much more I could have done on earth.— How differently would I have developed had I listened more to my inner self! I absorbed as much as I could from the outer world and sucked it up like a bee, but too seldom did I draw from my inner being. Much has escaped me by this negligence.

But I shall not complain; I thank my destiny for having given me in abundance during my short life on earth.

I can only be happy if you are also. I am making the greatest effort to advance you all further; therefore you must feel my nearness as an incentive to strive onward.

I can reach you better during the day. Then everything is clearer, within you also. I can be with you only when you are not influenced by strange fluids, and while you submerge yourselves in supersensible spheres.—It all works through the spiritual only, now that I have no body. Whenever you think of me you must think of my spiritual "I." All thinking about my bodily ego draws me back into the material, which is unpleasant.

God be with you all, you, whom I love so!

Karmicly I am closely connected with you, sister; you felt this more than I in my lifetime.

Sometimes, because I firmly believed in spiritual things, I was sad when some of you were cool when we spoke of them.

Now that I have departed from you, you wish ardently to know what happens after death, how it goes with me. This is understandable, but it is too bad we did not speak more about these spiritual matters while I was still on earth! It would all be less strange and far fetched for some of you. I feel we are very near each other, and this will become stronger the more you strive inwardly in this direction. Your lives will last a long time still. You will have more time to develop yourselves than I had. I submerged myself in the spiritual world only during the final two years of my life, all to the good for me now. I am thankful I had those

7

interests at the time. Of what use is erudition if man is ignorant of what happens after death!—Now I would—if I were still on earth—rather forego all earthly knowledge than be deprived of one thing: the faith in the future after death!—This is the fundamental thought and the sole truth; all else is a void in comparison.

I am following your various developments closely that I may know later how to guide you when it will be your turn to cross the threshold.

August 6, 1915

The battles that rage in the spiritual world are more intense than the war on earth, because the destruction of the spirit (of the individuality) is the issue here, whereas in your earthly war only the body is killed. Your world quiets down at night as ours stirs into activity. We have more time then to help the dead, who are streaming over to us by the thousands now.

How happy I was this afternoon; being with you all was so beautiful! I live the same way as on earth, except that I possess more capacities than I had in my physical body. I can divine much, but do not know everything by far; thus I have an intense desire to advance further. This desire is more effective here than when I was in a physical body, because one is more receptive. Otherwise, one is the same here as on earth. Whenever you are discussing questions concerning the supersensible world with persons highly developed spiritually, I also gain from it and learn through you what I cannot experience here. I cannot tell you much about this myself because I do not comprehend everything as yet. You can hardly understand this, therefore I always repeat it. To think the human being becomes perfect as soon as he lays his physical body aside is the greatest error. Your conversation today, for example, helped me exactly as much as it did you, even more so as I comprehend and understand quicker with my present senses, whereas the human brain often functions slowly. You must understand therefore that I am happy whenever you come together with such people as you did today because I can learn much and am closer to you on such occasions than in everyday life when you are busying yourselves with trivialities. I do not know how long I shall remain on this present spiritual level, but I believe it will not be much longer.—Then I shall step out of my present body just as you would lay aside your physical body.

You would surely like to know something of my life here. I am living only for the great task of which I spoke before, that is, the divine music, which will be of great benefit for mankind.—My work on earth was only a fraction of it. It will be something beautiful beyond measure that will penetrate all spheres and rise to the highest regions. One needs much strength and many talents for that. I felt I had to create something powerful. Therefore the calmness with which I went to war.—I knew that everything lies in God's hands. Not one moment's regret gripped me. It had to be, it was destiny! I always had the feeling that I should not grow old, but was not less joyful and content, tasting life in full measure because I knew that everything is foreordained and that I myself can alter nothing.

I was surprised, however, when death approached as I had not believed in it at the moment. During the long time I had been laid up, I had made plans for the future. The hope of returning home gave me courage and braced me up, although an inner voice kept saying, "Prepare yourself, you must step across."—I did not quite believe it, but then, suddenly, I saw my whole life before me and I knew that the end was near!—The last minute was terrible, but only for a moment and then it had passed, which means the sleep of death relieved me of all pain.

I had prepared myself for death unconsciously. My good karma had allowed me to repose for three weeks after my injury and to loosen myself gradually from the earthly sheaths. How much worse it is for those who die instantaneously since they cannot comprehend that death has overtaken them. Even I sometimes believed that I was still alive, because death is similar to living in the beginning. Thank God that I immediately became conscious of my discarnate condition. Then came the separation from the etheric body and I knew what had happened to me.

There followed the difficult task of calming you all and of making clear to you that I am still living.—This took much strength but you listened to me and lightened my effort, for which I thank you from my inmost depth. I shall never forget how you overcame yourselves for my sake. I shall reciprocate for it in time to come! I shall come to help you when you lay aside your bodies. This will be a joyous reunion!—Hold fast to that: This will continue to give you strength for overcoming your grief.

Please do not doubt but have faith that I shall continue to live as on earth, except that you cannot see me, and I am better off since I no longer have a body to carry.

I shall give you a verse:

> God has created the sun
> For the healing of mankind.
> The great sun of the Godhead reposes in us.

All His rays penetrate to heaven
From whence they have come.
In you rests the Divinity.
To seek Him is your duty.

We have conversed for a long time now without disturbances. It will and must succeed ever better, but you must have much quietness around you and not associate with too many different elements; these bring great unrest into your life and then I cannot penetrate to you.

August 7, 1915

I was deeply shaken and touched by what you read just now of my transmissions because I felt you were finally convinced that it is I who is speaking to you.
An unutterable happiness grips me when I am near to all of you with the knowledge that you are aware of me!
M., my sister, I have wanted to tell you something for some time; today I can as you are present also.—You helped me in the hour of death. Your nearness was a great comfort to me. Without your help my dying would have been much more difficult. I did not know how close you were to me in spirit.—Why did we not come near each other in life? You are such an introvert, but now we are intimately connected, helping each other.
My brother, I see your spiritual growth exactly. Whenever you work on yourself it seems as if a great, indestructible temple is transforming itself from a single small pillar. This is your ego, your spiritual "I"!
The bond that unites us is more intense now than during my lifetime because I can now be *within* you. I am

11

surrounding you with my help and love, and am able to protect you from ugly things that life on earth brings about.—Call me when you need me.—Your task is immense, but also beautiful and sublime; your path is illumined by the shining love of Christ's teaching.

The feeling of thankfulness toward all of you is growing steadily as I perceive how you are developing yourselves for my sake. I shall requite you for this in times hence!

August 8, 1915

Today was a great day for me! I have experienced much, have advanced by another degree, and have been admitted again into a high order to which I had belonged before but had been estranged from by my earthly incarnation. In this order I must fulfill my mission which I spoke to you about when on earth.—It pertains to music!—I have to create something higher than anything you would consider music.

Working is entirely different here. More intense, without technical complications and more difficult because it should represent the highest sublimity.—Something unfathomably great, beautiful, perfect! It will later also penetrate earthly realms, but only after a long time. Everything on earth has to be rebuilt now and guided in new directions.

I want to tell you of this work. I must compose a series of difficult symphonies. One is almost completed. You would be amazed to hear it, for this music is different from what I composed on earth, yet the fundamental theme is the same. I have to create seven symphonies in all, then the smallest part of this great symphonic work will be completed.

Others are working on it, too, but mine was a special task. This was waiting for me and was the reason for my early death. Do you comprehend now my happiness in being permitted to accomplish this?—The main purpose of it is to guide earthly sentiments into different channels. This music will merge into the various spheres surrounding the earth and will be powerful. You are unable to grasp, perhaps, how mankind could become more spiritualized by music, but it so. Music is the highest art; it alone can influence man indirectly. He hears and knows nothing of it because he occupies himself with earthly surroundings, and yet he must listen to this voice, which is us, *our work!*

You will be able to sense it when you have advanced several degrees. You cannot hear it yet but you will after death. I have received permission to perform it for you then. This is actually an exception as such great creations are only performed as a means to an end.

I can speak with you daily about new themes, and this work will grow gradually as "my gift" from this world to yours.

There was a festival today in which I took part.—A wonderful, an immeasurably tremendous festival! There were special combinations and melding of colors and tones, which had a deeply gripping effect and was so beautiful and perfect that one felt and played with the utmost enthusiasm.—This sounds incredible, but it is true!

Every thought that concerns me penetrates to me. This is

so beautiful! Even when I am far away, suddenly such a thought wings itself to me as a tender, lovely greeting from the physical world.

When one has had a few glimpses into the higher spheres, how great and glorious everything is! This is a strong incentive to advance further.—
We all have a certain path to tread, the question is which way to choose. We ourselves have to strive to find the right one. Should we choose the wrong one—which happens often—then there awaits us in the world beyond not punishment or reward according to the way we have lived, but we must travel the path of resignation because we had failed to choose the right way. Most go this way. I am happy you know the one you must travel.

I was also present at your music yesterday and I felt myself entirely in it. You must understand me rightly; I am present there and contribute by my nearness, unknown to you. All music has this close connection with me so that I am almost totally immersed in it. You should know by now what this means because I have said repeatedly, "I am with you," similarly I am "in the music" you are listening to.
I can barely write today because I have other work to do now also; therefore, I am divided. Formerly, this would have been impossible; now I need less strength.

Do not think I am guiding your hand; I hold it but I do not guide it. I am dictating every sentence that you have to write down; this is the procedure of my transmission. I must do my own work now.—God be with you all!

The mountains you admired were once my whole joy but now they lie farther away for me because I do not see them as singularly and as clearly before me. I am gazing into and beyond them now and that disturbs the uniform picture.

At any rate, the unrest over here is often terrible; too many and too varied elements are embattling and interpenetrating each other. It takes great will power to remain tranquil, but impatience succeeds even less. I can only look quietly into the distance with that one goal ahead of me.—That helps.—Do not think I really suffer under it, yet it is uncomfortable and disquieting.

The sun plays a great part here too. It provides the strength for all spiritual striving just as it also gave me the power for my work on earth. Its influence is tremendous, here and on the physical plane as well. It penetrates the physical much deeper than one imagines. One does not see the sun sometimes, but it is effective nevertheless. Accompanying it are the many planets, each exerting its own influence. This is all so unspeakably deep and great that one's amazement never ceases. I regret I have not developed further for perceiving it more clearly. The human brain can simply not comprehend the fullness of all that surrounds us and the earth. My will to know is becoming greater every day, and daily I am gaining more. A time has begun for all of you to see things in a different light. This is the first step. This is behind you; it proceeded faster than I dared hope. Everything you will need for your further advancement will now be given to you naturally. You will also become acquainted with people who will assist you further.—I cannot and dare not mix in, because it would mean interference with your karma (destiny); I am permitted merely to be with you, to listen in, console you, try to comprehend, give you strength: "That I live!" But I *must not* change anything in the path of life. This you will accomplish yourselves by your present way of thinking, through which you will create good things for your benefit.

I am speaking mainly about the time since my departure when your real life began. I may be around you, as I said, but I can interfere in nothing. Do not ask me for something I cannot give you.

Something else I want to tell you. Whenever you think of me, try to think of the spiritual Sigwart instead of the bodily one. This is not hard for you, and you will do me a great favor.

I have seen none of our acquaintances. I believe I shall find hardly any of them because no bond of love connects me with any of them; through such a bond only does one meet again!—The space we are in here is so immense, it is improbable to meet anyone by chance. How small is your earth in comparison!

I shall give you some words of wisdom. I heard them here and I have learned much from them. Please read them often and meditate on them.

> Hail to the eternal Godhead,
> Hail to the eternally invincible power
> Who penetrates *All,*
> Who surges through *All.*
> Eons of years have been,

Eons of years will come,—
Everything was, everything is—
And the eternal surf of life's oceans,
Which forever crashes against the cliffs of earth,
Will be calmed
By the Sun's holy, invincible power.

Faith is everything;
Without faith you are nothing.
Every plant has its faith,
Every beast its devotion.
And you, who are harboring the God within,
Will you deny Him and know better
What you are?
Great God, Who watches over the worlds,
Who guides and created all,
Have mercy upon me, who has trodden you under foot,
I, who believed myself to govern the world.
Great is your grace if you forgive me,
Since you are Love!
Therefore, I come to You and plead for mercy—
Yet this once forgive me!

Now I have found You;
I was weak—now I am strong
That I have found You from now on and forever.

This is a prayer that was given to me at the hour of death.—I felt how little I had recognized God. You must perceive God in everything, only then can you feel God gradually within yourselves. Before you have found Him within you, inseparable from you with every step, you will not comprehend the lofty messages I have been assigned to pass on to you.—

Please make the effort, try to understand, lest it be too late for us. It makes me unutterably happy to be the one who may initiate you all into these splendors.—My feeling of gratitude toward you is increasing daily. Such love I have not deserved; I shall reciprocate when the time comes! My thankfulness pertains to the work that is gradually developing through you, Sister, for all of you, but you must search for it in the profoundest depths. This will need a long time, as not everything can be expressed clearly, but can only be indicated symbolically.

I want to tell you a little story today:

Once upon a time there was a little ugly man, an atheist who wanted to convince the whole world of his teaching. —A great, handsome man came to him and said,

"How far do you want to spread your teaching?"

"Into the deepest depths of the earth," he replied.

"Well," said the beautiful one, "that is not dangerous at all, I thought you meant to reach beyond the earth."

"No," said the little ugly one, "there it is too bright for me."

"But what do you expect to achieve underneath the earth with your doctrine?" asked the handsome being.

"I simply want to disintegrate the whole earth with my doctrine, so mankind will finally comprehend that I am right."

"There is no danger in that, my dear," said the great one, "everything you break up is permeated by the one Divinity! Even if you annihilate the earth, it still exists in God."

So it is with God's teaching, should one try to destroy it.

The one who wants to annihilate it is actually promoting it.

You have transformed your grief for me into a great power, and through this power I can come to you.—This is such a joy for me! You are now at the beginning of that spiritual maturity that you shall achieve on earth.
I became a different human being during my last two years on earth, because I found inner self-recognition. Therefore I was calm, happy, and surrendered myself to my fate, for I *knew* and *believed*. Passing away and rebirth, all that had become clear to me. The truth had penetrated me;—and now I see you also feel the significance of it all, the reason it all happens the way it does,—then the divine calm overtakes you.

Sometimes I would like to tell you things I do not understand myself sufficiently. Then I beg my Helpers; they dictate it to me, and I pass it on to you. I am fortunate in this respect because I am surrounded by such Helpers who teach me as often as they can. This also is a good feature of my karma because this happens seldom. I am able to experience more this way in a shorter time than is otherwise possible for departed souls.—How happy I am over your comprehension of my present existence, even though I feel you still have momentary doubts whether it is I who speaks to you. I understand, it takes time to attain the faith that moves mountains. But this, too, will come about.

19

I was present in a Lodge today where I have heard and learned much. It exists on your earth, but I am forbidden to name it. It was very beautiful;—it belongs to the greatest on earth. I was led there to participate in something. It is a deep and earnest community, all members are highly developed individualities. Also many of us spiritual beings were present. The Lodge is not in Europe but in Mauretania,—I am not allowed to say more. You will hardly find the name on an ordinary map. It is a historical place, every educated person would recognize it.

I would like to give you a little prayer today; I learned of it when some doubts assailed me and I had pleaded for enlightenment:

> Softly my prayers rise on wings
> Of love to the light,
> Softly You wrap my limbs
> In the ether's
> Luminous raiment.
> Once only show me, Holiest God,
> The power of Your heavenly gaze,
> Help me to rise high on pinions,
> To behold *You,*
> Once only, my God!
> At your beholding I merge myself wholly.—
> Deep in Your Highest,
> Deep in my ego.

This turned out to be different perhaps than was intended, but it is difficult to form such mantrams in words; you must understand I need no words here where I only feel the sense of it. I have to transform these prayers into words for you to understand.

August 12, 1915

The verse I wish to give you now is for the ones who advance too rapidly:

> Wait—Wait—Wait!
> Think, practice, guide.—
> Be prepared
> For the time,
> Nothing too early,—
> Without stress,
> Everything must change,
> It lies in God's hand.

Dearest Mother!

Your son Sigwart is speaking to you. I have seen your pain and sorrow and I have suffered unutterably, but you have overcome yourself. You have grown in stature for my sake,—for that I thank you, my dearest good Mother. I know what I have to thank you for, a life full of sun and love. You had forgotten yourself in your self-sacrificing devotion. A rich crop has sprouted out of your selfless love, which is permeating your life.

You are so great, so strong, so mature. Yes, my dearest Mother, is it not wonderful,—I can and may continue to be united with you as long as I do not advance to higher regions, but I have still time left.

And now a greeting from the spiritual world:

Rivers of love flow yonder to the oceans of
    the Godhead.
Every prayer out of the depth of the heart
Awakens a flowerlet in Father-God's meadow.
You are the love,
You were the light.
In you the divinity,
Above you the eternal changes of time.
Believe and pray,
Step gratefully over the threshold of earth
Yonder to the altar of Light.
Great and omnipotent are you,
The heavenly calm filled with humility
Resting within you—
Blossoming around you,
In eternity,
Always!

I want to tell you why I never speak about the grave.—
You see, I do not want to contribute anything to my
corpse. Every thought about it adds a force for its
survival. It must disintegrate without any strength being
added. It is my old body, fully estranged now, therefore I
do not wish to think about it anymore.
I linger often at the beautiful place beneath the oak tree
because I always loved it, but I never think of my remains
below the soil, feeling only happiness surrounded by your
love.
My transitory remains are of no value, only the thoughts
you create there where they lie. Not one thought should
linger below the soil. Do not allow yourselves to nourish
my corpse with your thoughts! Help me to build a temple
of consecration; then we shall always meet there,—but

only in that way, otherwise I cannot stay at that place. Only your noble thoughts beckon me there, not the mourning that I cannot bear.

August 15, 1915

Beloved Father!
Your son is speaking to you!
I know you believe in my present existence, therefore I need not convince you of it. Yet I must convince you that *your son Sigwart* is speaking to you!

I have been permitted to converse with you in this way, and I am indescribably happy about it.

I know how much we meant to each other in life, how much we treasure each other now, and I am attached to you with the most ardent love.
I departed from you because I had greater tasks to fulfill. Everything was prepared for me, therefore do not grieve for me because I have been chosen for a holy work. I have been called upon to create a part of it. This has to do with music. Seven heavenly symphonies are being composed! One of them I have completed.—It is the purpose of these works to guide the impulses on earth into purer channels. The music will accomplish that. It will act upon humanity indirectly. This is our strongest medium for influencing mankind.
I have seen your beloved mother, she has suffered with you in your sorrow; she has surrounded you with her unending love, which never ceases, and she is as much around you as only a mother can be around her child. She

begs you never to think of her in sorrow. You have hurt her by mourning for her. One may not grieve for a departed one. We remain united exactly as on earth, although the bereaved ones are not able to perceive it. You cannot imagine what it means to us who no longer have physical bodies when someone we love weeps for us. This is the most severe anguish for us to endure because we still feel exactly as we did on earth. How your mother would have suffered while still alive had she seen you so sad. She could not have endured it,—and yet she must bear it now!—We feel every thought of pain the same as we did in our earthly state because we are the ones you knew and loved. Grieving creates a chasm between you and us. Later only love remains—the highest, holiest and most intimate bond. This I should tell you from her. She will welcome you when your hour has come.

How happy I am to have your support,—I knew that you would eventually come to believe that it is I who am speaking to you.—If you had seen me yesterday as I stood next to you, listening to your explanation of my messages, you would have become as radiantly happy in your heart as I was.—You have no need to see me, you know and sense me enough, and for this I thank you, my dear Father. A calm has come over you that will remain with you until we see each other again.

Life is short and eternity so beautiful! You have faith, a faith that moves mountains. This is a blessing for me, for your loved ones, and also for yourself.

Your forever faithful son Sigwart sends you a greeting from the spiritual world.

> The currents of love are immense
> That surge through you, oh man,

24

Son of God!
Father of light and love, Ruler
of death are You
And of tranquility.
Inconceivable is Your might,—and You gave
Of it to me.
And now I conceive fully Your might,
That watches over me.
Now I can endure, even
Though the world should crumble.
Only this thought survives:
I am—You are!

August 18, 1915

I can come so near to you sometimes that I can feel you
bodily.
I can squeeze your hand, but you cannot feel it.
You must never forget that a bond of love between human
beings endures eternally. Years are of no significance,
nothing can sever it. How short a span of time is your life
compared to eternity! You have different concepts of
time, therefore let nothing trouble you: There exists no
separation for those who were united by the bond of love
during life on earth.

August 21, 1915

Today was a wonderful day. I listened to music, the most
lofty, the most heavenly melodies I have ever heard. I
participated in it, as I had all the threads in my hand and

perceived audibly everything in its most delicate nuances. My longing to hear this music was so strong that I was granted to be present. It has caused a profound ecstacy in me. I cannot describe what I have experienced. The glow of this holy harmony is still permeating me, and I thank the Highest One for letting me hear it!

I know you are unable to comprehend it, but it is so. I, too, have gloomy moments sometimes; then I have good friends at my side who have gone through these phases before. They help me with mantrams with which I have to merge myself completely. Praying in this sense only helps here. I shall pass on some of the verses to you for your benefit.

August 22, 1915

Beloved Sister!

I come to you today to thank you. The currents of your love that steadily flow to me are engulfing me completely. I feel every thought you are sending to me, and I hear every note you are playing for me. I am happy because you all have overcome yourselves.

I am in the midst of all of you since then. When you are happy I am near you. I cannot bear your sorrow, I had suffered too much in the beginning, because I loved you all. As you have mastered your pain by playing for me I was guided into the quiet pathway of your music, which comforted me immensely. These mild, lovely gifts filled me with restfulness, which returned slowly after I had passed the initial terrible chaos.

The compositions I had created on earth are being

performed here also. These are a small fraction of a mighty work which is indescribably overpowering.

When I perceived this I knew why I had to part from you. My job was waiting for me: this is the great mission I have mentioned before. If only I could tell you more about it, but you would be unable to comprehend it. Some time hence you will understand and feel it yourself. This thought pleases me very much. I love you, as always, your Sigwart.

A great power lies in every human being, but how few use it rightly. This is their greatest fault: their vanity predominates so much; this must be eliminated, only then does one perceive the real goal. I know it is difficult for you, nevertheless, you must overcome this weakness if you want to aspire to the highest.

Begin with the smallest attempt, try to prevail over one thing at a time, and then over two a day,—until you have gained a certain strength by often reviewing the results during the day. Later you will have to watch out for every vain thought that begins to stir.

I have heard your conversation.—I also have the same sentiments and I often long to be physically united with you all. Those are the only moments when I need help, and then I receive mantrams and prayers that assist me to overcome it. Such desires will disappear gradually, but it takes time.

I suffer often with you even though I do not mention it; these pains are different here, however, and are not as intense as yours. Therein lies the burden of earthly life, namely, by being imprisoned within matter. Yet I believe the hope of seeing me again will console you.

All of us who love each other had the wonderfully good fortune of having been closely connected as relatives in the present life. We were together in this way for the first time, and it will probably repeat itself in the future, unless one of us commits a crime, which I do not expect, however!

I have severed the bodily bonds that connected us, and this was very hard, yet one of us had to make a beginning. Now that the bond is rent on earth, a new one is already being woven, more beautiful and intimate than the former one. This connection will become an ever more ardent one with each death and rebirth, until neither death nor life can separate us. Therein lies the greatness of continued development, the nucleus of which is *love*. Can you understand now how everything else is insignificant compared to this love that lasts forever?

I have heard your question:

I am not in the so-called "Astral Sphere," nor in the "Devachan Sphere" at present, but in a middle realm. I have advanced farther in a shorter time than many others because of my interest in everything spiritual during my life on earth.

August 23, 1915

You are wondering why I have never spoken directly about the war. But so much unrest, sorrow, despair and fear is part of it that I dislike to occupy myself with it. The enthusiasm is missing here with which the people on earth are intoxicating themselves in order to be able to bear all the misery.—There one refuses to see the ugliness and

28

sadness, but one cannot escape it over here. The chaos, all the pain and misery, the confusion of sentiments is terrifying here.

I do not join the battles anymore as many still do. I have other work to do, as you know.

The war itself is of such a cruel nature, every thought of it pains me.—You should not forget I see so much more now than you do. One experiences all cruelty and terror from two sides. One perceives not only the suffering of the body, but also the tortured spirit.—This is too much; therefore I occupy myself with the war for the purpose only of alleviating some of the pain. This does not mean that my dying was also horrible.

My death was beautiful, everything became still, it changed to a quiet, calm sea after a blustering storm. The final experiences as man were part of this storm, then came the smooth waters of liberation. I would have parted from you at any rate, you may believe that.—I had not been destined for old age. It was a blessing to have been freed without illness, without extended pining away. Be as thankful for it as I am because it was the best way to die;—my death was the most perfect of its kind.

August 30, 1915

The foundation stone of the great temple of consecration has been laid at my grave by the overcoming of your sorrow. Now I can be with you completely. Everything fell on fertile soil, and this eases even more the communication with you. I shall be able to initiate you soon into specific things because you are all working together. You

are creating a power through your conviction that allows
me to impart to you many things I could not have done
before.

Please recite this prayer at the place of consecration:

Great is the Lord of the worlds, Who
Created you and called you back to Him.
Here I stand at the consecrated place
And pray to You.
All matter vanishes, all sublimity endures—
Your wings are spread, receiving Your child.
All redemption is holy becoming,
Death mere transition—all else fulfillment!
Let me behold You, Father of mine,
Whose will is all-encompassing.
Receive me to Your Self, open the heaven of Yours!
At last the time has come, and You, my God, are near me.
How glorious is death when You are with me.

September 5, 1915

I want to tell you about my present life:

I have reached a sphere where everything is easier; I am
less disturbed by many things that used to confuse me. An
oscillation of equanimity surrounds me.

My work is also more satisfying here because it is freer
from your earthly influences. The difference is as day and
night. The day is bright, the night dark, and now I am
working as in daytime.

Also, I am removed from your petty worries since I
ceased to partake in them, which used to torment me.
Naturally, every strong sentiment concerning myself pene-

trates to me, but I am less bothered by the hundreds of little troubles and thoughts. I can be of much greater value to you now as I have greater power to expend. Communication with you is proceeding better also. This I had to learn from the beginning.

I cannot dispose of myself as much from here as I could earlier. The transitions from level to level are hardly noticeable, less so than you would surmise. We barely feel the difference. Believe in me, *please,* you are my sole help and support. Therefore believe it is I, *Sigwart,* who loves you all. I understand that you have sometimes thoughts of doubt. You see, death came too suddenly for me, otherwise I would have prearranged for possible means of intercourse with you. I know the experience of unhappiness now if one wishes to speak to the beloved ones, yet they cannot hear. This is agony!

As I can see through this dilemma, I advise each one of you fervently to talk this over with your beloved ones on earth, lest the one who is called away first will have to suffer the same torment. How much easier it would have been for me had I spoken up beforehand; my approach would have been experienced as quite natural, and your faith firm from the first. I have almost finished the seventh symphony. It was a difficult yet an exhilarating task. Everything is ready for the great moment of performance. A new life is commencing for me, the life of "reposing in oneself." I meditate by immersing myself completely in my ego. Nothing of unrest is allowed to penetrate from outside; it is a kind of contemplation that requires absolute solitude.

Therefore our communication will be different from now on; I may still continue to write, but of spiritual concerns only.

New doors are opening for me; I may behold glorious sights.—Have I not reason to be happy? As we can no longer see each other on the physical plane, it is more satisfying to advance as quickly as possible and explore all the splendor.

If only you could see! Would your eyes were not fettered by matter! What is all the beauty on earth compared to the glory and perfection here! Your earthly joys are as the joys of little children, who only perceive a formless mass and grasp for it without understanding what it is. They cannot think, and comprehend nothing, and if the most beautiful landscape is shown them they would see naught. Now I can look through all this and I am fully aware of the spirit's confinement on the physical plane.

September 6, 1915

I, Sigwart, died for you also in order to show you the path to the spirit.

Here is a mantram which will help you. Immerse yourselves in it:

> Yes, Father, I give my spirit to you completely.
> Yes, Father, I fulfill completely whatever You wish.
> Receive me, that I may become strong
> To fulfill the holy work You gavest me to do.

September 7, 1915

I have learned much today.—How hard it is to persevere in being immersed completely in oneself, but it was my

32

decision. I have renounced further immediate contact with you because I saw an abyss before me from which it would have been difficult to extricate myself.

Now *you* have to follow me lest the distance between us will become too great. Therein lies the marvel of our love—that you approach to meet me, not the reverse. You are helping me to advance for which I thank you all, my beloved ones. It usually proceeds in the opposite direction; the departed soul helps those left behind and is thus hindered in his further development. In the beginning I sent only as much help to you as lay in my power; now you have been supporting me for some time. This will take us to the goal for we are advancing together. So much is happening within all of you of which you are unaware, but I can see it!—This occurs in each one of you differently. Ah, my beloved ones, if only we were united again!

Mighty are the laws of Providence. We must submit to them. These are laws of *iron!* But when we obey them with fortitude and humility they are delightful and wondrous. The chain that unites it all is forged under the loving eyes of our Father. This should becalm you; persevere in this humble station until the hour of our reunion.

As ever in love and gratitude, your Brother.

September 8, 1915

I have sensed your sentiments toward me. You need not fear your mourning might influence me aversely. Not anymore. Such thoughts are bound to appear as long as we are human beings. I am not as sensitive to them as in the beginning. This is the advantage of continuous development. Gradually purely spiritual thoughts reach us only, then we advance serenely, unhindered by disturbances.

You have to imagine me in a different light now because I have changed completely. Yet all thoughts of love still reach me. Whenever you are thinking of me consider also your own development. You have to advance with that one goal before you.

It is up to you now, I have done all in my power. We shall not succeed without your cooperation. But, needless to say, you will follow me even if the path is rigorous, for your love is great and strong.

Let everyone read this in order that they, too, may become aware that the time for real effort is now. *I* gave you the strength so far, now the vigor must come out of yourselves. Be grateful that I am allowed to tell you this lest I see you ignorantly plunge down the high mountain my power and love has helped you to ascend. Now you know my situation, so act accordingly.

Here is another mantram, meditate on it often:

> I am—and You in me.
> I was—and You near me.
> I will—and *You are mine.*

September 9, 1915

How long the process of dying lasts!—I am still dying; I am divesting myself continuously of sheaths, and each time I perceive more and feel differently. Only my love for

34

you remains the same; it penetrates *everything* because it is unchanging and eternal.

My *true* life has begun now; the dream condition has ended, and yet, compared to your lives, this phase is the more positive. How sad that life on earth is perpetually enveloped in mist. One sees nothing, feels even less, and the little tormenting worries of daily life add to it all. Nevertheless, the longing for an earthly incarnation persists among us; therein lies progress. Otherwise, the spirits would hardly decide to descend repeatedly into the bodily prison had not the desire and joy for it been put into their hearts.

September 12, 1915

I have overcome most of the hardships now, I have passed a test. It was not easy, but then the feeling of success is *glorious.*

Great is the goodness and justice of our Father!—Now I know the reason for my death. I must create something great—a mighty work of music—and it is my mission to spread the sublime teachings through you, within an intimate circle first, and then beyond. I am also to help you to understand and bear your destiny without sorrowing because suffering diminishes with comprehension. Finally, my death was a new birth of our love. Are these not splendid reasons? Does this not console you fully? The period of self-contemplation has ended. Part of my ego is still occupied with it, but for a few hours I may enjoy again the pleasures of sublime existence.

The fetters of earth have been stripped off me. You wonder why it happened so soon. Yet it is no fantasy that

my so-called "Hero's death" has something to do with it. The soldiers who sacrifice their lives with unselfish enthusiasm have it easy here. However, they have to be filled exclusively with the impulse, "I am doing my duty!" This is a wonderful preparation for the heavenly life.
God protect you all!

September 13, 1915

Even though I continue to progress I am always present and know how you are. We meet together in everything profound, be it in art, in prayer, or in the beauty of nature, it is all the same. I still feel every great thought. You have to understand that I am able to maintain our connection from every sphere because the loftiest, purest love is uniting us, and it will endure eternally, you must believe me!
Rejoice with me when I tell you I have advanced again, for every divesture is a festival.

As I was with all of you tonight I could see how falling asleep is related closely to dying. Material existence clings to the spiritual by a thread, and the spirit rejoices in being free. We then converse with each other just as in life on earth, and I tell you much of myself. But you must not miss the moment of return to your physical bodies. All this proceeds according to exact laws that human beings obey unconsciously. On awakening your spirit is fully earth-bound again and you know nothing of our togetherness, although you resolve each time to try to remember. You can only achieve this when you have advanced far

36

enough to meet me consciously in sleep. I think some of you will still reach this state on earth.

I told you much about my life and death tonight. You all surrounded me in a circle and we rejoiced in the long duration of the gathering. Perhaps the memory will awaken suddenly if I repeat the story each time. It may appear as a dream at first, but it is always myself who is with you in sleep.

September 15, 1915

The Spirit is watching over your progress, divine strength is filling your soul, warm rays of light are penetrating you. Your "I" is abiding on the summit of the holy mountain anticipating the bright rays of the sun. These will anneal you like molten gold, so, when bowed in humility, your soul's eyes will behold the celestial purity.

September 18, 1915

I was far away from you today, attending to a pleasant task. I had to instruct ignorant pupils and was able to show them splendid proofs of the transition of souls to immortality. They were soldiers recently killed in the war whose faith had not been very strong during their lifetime; they were quite open to accepting my teachings. It meant much effort but I liked to do it as I had pity on their ignorance. It is different with those who deny everything and *refuse* to believe. There the work is rather unpleasant as feelings of resentment are apt to arise in one. Such

37

sentiments are strictly forbidden to us teachers, however. I am glad I have learned to suppress such feelings. When I see now how your life is confined and depends on thousands of things I am happy to have overcome it all, inasmuch as you are not tormenting me anymore with thoughts of pain and doubt.

The threads of our love are becoming ever more intimate and beautiful. We are actually bound by invisible threads, therefore the subtle reciprocating responses. Naturally, this is easier from my side as I do not have a physical body and sense every vibration immediately. With you it has to penetrate the many dense layers, and you do not feel all my gentle sentiments and expressions of feelings.

Few people know that an actual connection, fostered by great love, exists between the living and the dead.

September 20, 1915

I shall give you a poem today that can help you much:

> I have the will to reach for the highest.
> I shall succeed.
> Forgive me for my weakness.
> But I know You are coming to me,
> Therefore it will leave me.
> Help me, most Sublime One, Allmightiest!
> Your will is my will,
> I bow myself before You.

Destiny ordained that I should depart before you because I could be of more help to you in my spiritual state. I believe none of you would have received permission to spread the divine teaching. This privilege I credit to my life before last when I strove to investigate the spiritual world but had little opportunity to do so.

But now, in this last life, the supersensible realms lay open to me; my faith had become so strong through the previous desire that I had no need to search for it much. I often had the feeling of a holy overshadowing in the last years of this incarnation. I had felt an indefinite presentiment of something divine flowing through me and immersed myself fully in it.

In those moments I longed for redemption, for freedom, for I divined how beautiful these might be, and I knew I had few passions left to overcome. I was never afraid of death.

Now that I have divested myself of all material sheaths I may tell you there are quite unpleasant moments to be gone through after death. Fortunately, I was able to collect myself in perfect quietness; otherwise it would have been difficult to extricate myself from the chaos. Helpers and good friends stood by me with advice, which gave me the necessary inner tranquility.

September 21, 1915

I can tell you much today near this beautiful sea. Such a pure atmosphere here. I can see into the depths of the ocean, everything in it and what it consists of. Amazingly mighty and glorious are all these miracles above and below the earth. Everyone of us can see these things according to the hundreds of steps of development, because the impulse and wish to "know" is as strong here as on earth, for every one of us feels there exists still higher sublimity yet undiscovered.

You may form a tiny concept of eternity if you imagine that I—with the knowledge I now have—feel like a timid little child who envisions something magnificent that is unattainable to him. Do you understand now the sentiments with which I think of you earth-bound ones? When I compare my experiences, what I comprehend and enjoy, it is quite natural for me to long for your liberation from these dense veils.

I am around you without the minutest longing for anything of material substance. Our connection is purely spiritual now.—It was different in the beginning when I experienced the same sentiments then as I had in life on earth. Every proximity with you called forth the desire for incarnation; I was still young when I had to divest myself of the body; this makes a great difference. If one dies as a child or in old age these feelings are usually absent.

I see you more distinctly now: akin to a perception and divining of everything sublime and spiritual in you. Every emotion causes vibrations around you, and I feel your love accordingly. It is the same with colors, which, to my regret, you do not wear. White is pleasant and nice, but I prefer colors. Black is awful! It is not worthy of you to wear it considering your present spiritual attitude.

At the place of consecration where I often linger now, there are colors I love that provide joy for me.

I am creating fabulous impressions through color games. If you only could see that, I believe you would never forget it!

September 23, 1915

The roof upon your house
Is blessed,
Roses are growing upward on the walls . . .
And eyes of longing are gazing
From the windows.
Wait awhile!
Open your hearts to the waves
Of Divine Grace,
And a light will be enkindled for you
That will never be extinguished.
It brightens your works by day,
And your experiences by night.
Thus Divine Love embraces you
And you are resting protected in His lap.
The Lord blesses you.

How all things have been illuminated! The streams of
your lives have left the old channels and are flowing in a
different direction.

It was well-ordained that I depart from you. Had I
returned from the war you would never have changed.
You had to go through this sorrow. Your lives will still
last long, but the time for insight is short. I trembled for
you in the beginning, wondering whether you could bear
the pain in dignity; for had you not overcome yourselves,
our bond of love would have been severed. But we need
not fear any more now. Everything will proceed along
proper ways and a most glorious reunion is certain for us.
You will see how a web of the purest and noblest
spirituality will be woven around you. Your being abides

within this fine net, and your proximity is felt as a comfort by the outside world.

Human beings have no idea how effective mutual influences are. The so-called vibrations are the result of spiritual attributes, which are transmitted to your contemporaries as sympathy or love—infinitely comforting, stimulating and encouraging for self-improvement. You will sense that yourselves, and in time you will exert great influence on your fellowmen.

September 25, 1915

Death is not extinction, but resurrection; life is not a becoming, but annihilation. The structure of matter must be shattered in order to liberate the force gained by the spirit during life. As long as matter prevails, spirit remains anchored within it. When the matter returns to nature, *that spiritual force remains* because it is different from nature's and cannot be dissolved in it. Then the spirit searches for what earthly life has preserved for it—and finds that *force!*

The spirit, strengthened by it, begins the ascent toward the heights. This force is of multiple kind and form. It arises like the precipitation of crystals from all that man achieves and creates by his efforts on earth. Spiritual currents move through even the most materialistic endeavors, and with the sweat of his brow man must shape these currents into what he calls his works. The soul that enlivens his works is the force man has created; it endures beyond his earthly body and becomes the ladder on which man's liberated spirit ascends to perfection.

At the place of consecration!

How beautiful it is here! The peace, the quiet of it, and of the world of sublime thoughts that here forms a temple of purest web. Could you but read my prayers often here, could you but see how only in such moments all the great, pure and lofty spiritual beings come to you and surround you! They all experience comfort in your nearness and spread this calm about you. The great power reaches farther now. In its center the concentrated thoughts build the foundations of the temple. You have worked whole-heartedly in this way: for this I thank you all again and again.

Some unrest surrounds you today that makes it difficult for me to converse with you. I can succeed only when complete peace is within and around you. Should I find no echo because of lack of harmony, I am permitted to relate only half of what there is to say and my Masters tell me that I am casting sublimity to the winds!

The work belongs to you, to each one of you—and should serve other purposes later on as well.

I heard your conversation yesterday evening. How beautiful it is when you meet and discuss spiritual questions. I answer you then—often you perceive it but sometimes not. I can see how immensely instructive this hour is for all of you, just as I can see the effect in each one of you. It is not only our circle that gathers, but many others join in who exchange their opinions and teach themselves, me, and you.

If you continue to read and occupy yourselves with spiritual things, doing it always at the same hour, a powerful force will develop in the future because higher

43

beings are taking part who influence you, and thereby help to solve the most difficult questions for you.

I am closest to you in this hour and in time I shall be able to make myself ever more noticeable according to the greater force that will be at my command. Even if you feel me bodily, do not think I shall be pulled downward; not anymore, for I have risen above that.

September 27, 1915

I shall give you a few thoughts in prose:

"You are asking about our life here, oh man. You cannot comprehend it, for everything around you and within you is sealed in tightly. Yet there is one way to behold the splendor and to find the world of secrets, so hear:
Every thought concerning God steps outside the circle of confinement and becomes free.
Every thought about eternity tears itself loose and will break out of the prison of earth-enwrapped matter.
Every thought of love begets wings, flying outward and upward, ever so high! There above, in the regions of light, such thoughts meet again, unite closely and ascend together.
They are not free as yet, however, because from the hearts of men down below, from these little hearts, grow three threads spun of gold, reflecting the lustre of the sun.—
They are spun ever so long, for the power of conviction gives a helping hand. They are never torn asunder, they hold fast, alas, ever so fast. They are pulled through everything until the heart of man can no longer abide below. This heart struggles with itself for awhile, with the

44

earthly force of life, but one ardent wish suffices—and free it has become. And now the self-created thoughts raise him upward by the golden threads to the eternal sun!"
You see, it is also the same with faith. Every really lofty thought arising from the Godhead lifts the human being out of the bodily sheath and gives him the power and desire to become free. The human soul is thus raised and lifted upward by the threads of its own thoughts. Therefore, *thoughts* are import, not deeds. Thoughts play the greater part; one can achieve everything with them, whereas deeds are limited. Remember this, and you will advance yourselves in easier stages.

You have opened your doors. The more your faith increases, the nearer you will be to me; you must yet learn more, but do not let this discourage you. You must reach your goal and fulfill your calling.

September 29, 1915

T., dear Sister, I have blessed you with the fervor of my heart. How near you are to me! I shall welcome you here with open arms when you come to me. You are my gentle sun, whose rays you are sending to me from far distances. The chains that bind us are subtle and eternal.
You ascended the high mountains to seek me, and you found me steeped in silent contemplation, alone on the holy summit. I awoke as you softly touched my hand. You came to fetch me back to life because you needed me. This occurred before my last incarnation.
Your desire to be born with me again, to spend a new life with me, was so strong that you succeeded in calling me

back before my time. Thus you forged this close connection through the ardency of your wishes and prayers.

October 2, 1915

Your lives have become rich, and that is a great joy for us here. In comparison, how depressing is the sight of the average human beings who crowd in on the spiritual world. What a relief when suddenly one of them shines with the reflection of divine brilliancy, but it happens very seldom.

Billions of mediocre souls are closest to your earth. The attraction the earth exerts upon these souls is amazing and comparable to a magnet. An indefinitely long time will have to pass before this effect will cease. The undeveloped part of the earth has this magnetic pull on the surrounding world of souls. The earth is permitted to attract only those souls who, because of their stage of development, are forced to descend into matter again; others it has to repel. Fortunately, I am not being drawn into this magnetic vortex anymore, and thus I am now able to survey it all. Through God's grace I was able to rise above it from the moment my real higher existence began. There is much to be learned, always and everywhere. I am called upon to be of true help to you. Thank God for it.

October 3, 1915

The hour of consecration! I bless you and have my being in you—you are helping us, you are helping yourselves, you are helping the Godhead Who is watching over you.

Legions of light-beings gather here at the place of dedication. Have you not felt them? You already perceive all this distinctly. First you feel it; later you will see it.

I have heard you sing and I have recognized the old familiar themes. Every note tells me something, a whispering of precious times when we were united. A longing is hidden therein, deeper than remembrance.

Come often and bring lofty thoughts for me! It is your task to build the magnificent temple. Every profound thought is a building stone, and infinitely numerous ones are needed. Give me—present me with many building stones!

October 4, 1915

I experienced something indescribably beautiful today. Great impressions that are hard to explain were transformed into intermingled sounds and colors. We understood the meaning of it at once, but for others here it was a riddle. These are pleasant sensations, which also test one's capacity to comprehend such impressions, since they demand strict concentration. I cannot explain to you to what extent the effects will become incarnated, because your concepts are inadequate for understanding it. Everything in our world is so totally distant from your logic, and from the premises human brains have concocted with the so-called sharp intellect. Only feelings and sentiments contribute to comprehension here. You see, it is a totally different conception to judge everything by the capacity of comprehending through higher feelings alone. The more a spirit is developed, that much more readily will his soul react to all external impressions. This is so rich and proliferous. What blissfulness when one feels about, and reacts accurately to, something one had ignored previously. It is my task to achieve this at the moment. I must make myself more sensitive in order to convince others through my experiences. Average human beings let themselves be converted even here only by actual proofs. They, too, do not listen to the inner voice that speaks to them. Blessed are they who believe without proof!

October 5, 1915

I can be with each one of you simultaneously whenever I wish to. Speaking pictorially, I am holding the spiritual thread of life of each one in my hand and for this reason I am connected intimately with all of you. It is more pleasing for me, of course, when you are gathered in a circle, it requires no effort then on my part.

Work diligently in your gardens of life so that new shining flowers may sprout everywhere. Nurse them along, for through love and faithful patience only will the garden of glorious flowers slowly blossom.

You should live and terminate your lives in gentle wingings of flight. Remember this whenever worry enshrouds your head in the course of life, then will anxiety bow before you.

The time will come when divine peace shall embrace you all, and will not send you back into the unrest of the earth.

October 7, 1915

A different period is approaching for you. You must work intensely on yourselves for our further enjoyment of such immediate communion. To remain in such direct intercourse with you is granted to me only because we are so close to each other, but especially because you reciprocate my effort.

You must continue to live in this way. Observe the hour of meditation, organize the day better, then you will reach the goal easier. Do not forget that I suffer more under disharmonies in our circle than before. I am struggling for peace with you in great and small affairs. Only harmony, unity and love will keep me in your midst. Should you fail in this I must then withdraw. The time will come when I shall not be allowed to communicate with you; this will test whether or not doubts will assail you, and if you will be able to continue to think of me with the same magnanimity. Much will depend on that, especially how our communication will shape itself later on.

October 10, 1915

I was allowed to influence you merely by standing at your side and assuring you again and again, "You must not mourn, I am beside you, I hear everything you say—I am alive!" It depended on you whether to believe or not believe. Any other proof was forbidden me. Otherwise I did as much as lay in my power. You understand me, you feel and hear me, therefore we can work differently and exactly now. Do you think I would have been permitted to tell so much from here if all of you had not developed yourselves also?—No, not half of it might have been related to you.

A communication such as ours between living and deceased ones happens very seldom. You cannot imagine how privileged we are due to our close connection and through your and my longing for everything sublime. I must beg you, however, to ask me whenever you intend to confide our messages to someone. Through some indiscretion on your part it could happen that I might lose permission to contact you again. This will change later.

October 14, 1915

The Masters are sending the truth to you through me in order that I may point the way and prepare your souls.
Submitting to the Highest,—this is the great secret of the irresistible way of becoming.
Most people do not sacrifice their forces in the service of the sublime; they want to penetrate it with the powers they possess, but do not know how.
All strength transforms itself to power only when it wills to become powerless itself by acknowledging the Higher Power above it.
    Everyone works in the service of higher beings and is also at the service of lower ones. It is the same with you and within you.—The ego, your own self, permeated by the Godhead, illuminates the denser sheaths of your being for the mutual ascent.
God, who has sent you forth, has laid the thought of eternity in your hearts through His incomprehensible might. You are divine, therefore, holy, and holy is the never changing, always enduring, never vanishing eternity, which serves even the Godhead Who created it.
You, too, are eternal; sink this highest of all thoughts deeply into your hearts, for out of God originated the eternity you feel in yourself.

October 17, 1915

I have blessed you all and have closed the circle that had to be welded for all eternity. It has great importance! Nothing can separate us any more. This last of the brazen bonds was forged in this hour. Now we have accomplished the *first* union,—others will follow.
Thank God for this gift, it is greater than any earthly goods.
Be humble in your faith, because He gave you something magnificent.
God be with you in all eternity.

October 18, 1915

I shall tell you a story:

When God created the world He thought of me also. He spoke to me thus: "Little man, you are the greatest on earth, everything is yours, but you must understand why. I am dwelling in your bodies, I, your God.—You have such variously fashioned raiments wherewith I want to adorn Myself. You have the sun to warm you. Your wings are large and reach up to my firmament, and they beat so softly that sea and earth are silent in order to listen. A cloud is enveloping you that is finer and brighter than the spheres' most radiant blue,—thus I am resting in you!
But why is it that after a long, long time has passed, and while your wings are still rustling and your cloud is shining brilliantly, you yourself are asleep?

51

Who gave you to drink of the waters of Lethe?

Oh, sleeping child of man, encompassed as you are by the great living spheres that rotate with the eternal wheel of the worlds, you have forgotten yourself and also Me. For see, you did not hold fast to my Might, which is greater than the earth. Yet there is life still in you; the covenant still exists.

Do not tear yourself away, do not plunge drowsily into the abyss of the eternal void."

I feel your thoughts as waves emanating from you. The most sublime thoughts are the brightest and gentlest sounding ones. Indifferent thoughts cause opaque and insignificant waves. Except for really evil ones that you do not have, thoughts of unrest are the worst, and I perceive them as a stormy sea that battles and surfs against itself. Such thoughts spread the unrest further into the spiritual spheres.—Whenever the brightly sounding waves flow toward me I am drawn to them at once. Bad thoughts create a spiritual force that accompanies man as a separate being.

You experience and penetrate your world only with your physical eyes, which presents a mere reflection of the true world. Whatever shows itself as proof through the veil of material existence—can that satisfy you?

Open the eyes of your soul and the portals of your faith.—Therein lies the truth. Seek there and you shall become wise.

You surely know how deceptive the reliance on such proofs is. How poor would be the one who has investigated all the evidence of your world, but were ignorant of the source of it! What a sad work of fragments this would be and how far from harboring the *truth* within it.

So believe and accept, as the tree believes in the light of the sun without seeing it, only sensing it, lifting its branches longingly skyward and spreading its twigs like a net wherein to receive the blessings of the Creator. First to believe, then to see! First to feel,—then to become the chalice of revelation, wherein the Creator can mirror Himself in its clear waters.

We still deceive ourselves in many ways here concerning our world, but we are able to search quickly for the errors and recognize them provided we seek for them humbly. You were disappointed because I had failed to understand correctly one of your questions. I listen with fullest devotion and assist you with all the forces of my love for our mutual contact. The communication is inadequate sometimes because your questioning thoughts are not strong enough to reach me as a distinct language. Is it not conceivable that we can err when we have to transpose ourselves suddenly into your world? Through love only, by the greatest effort, do we attain the capacity to recognize the intent of your questions.

We are neither omniscient nor perfect; we are freed spirits who try to absorb the knowledge of this world. The more we adopt ourselves to the sphere we belong to, the farther are we removed from your world.

You say that "erring is human," but I say to you that whatsoever calls itself "being" and not "God" is subject to deception and is incapable of comprehending correctly.

October 19, 1915

Be silent, for your silence is akin to outspread wings, under whose protection I scatter shining blossoms into your hands. They may not wilt, nor may frost carelessly destroy their splendor.

Their pollen will be carried upward by your faith to a sanctuary that everyone harbors as a core in his being.

There, in your flower garden, the most glorious blossoms will unfold.

The seeds of *these* plants only you are allowed to entrust to the effervescent children of spring when the time has come.

Struggle for your equanimity, for the peace in you, so no storm or frost will destroy your little garden.

October 23, 1915

(In March 1915, while still alive, Sigwart had written to an old friend, "I have not developed myself away from but rather toward Parsifal. I feel him as my native home, as my profession of faith.")

I was present at the explanation of Parsifal; I have to disagree with some of it, although my friend has interpreted the depth of it correctly.

The basic thought pertains to Christ's blood, which has *actually transformed* the astral substance of the earth. Right after this occurrence events took place in the various layers surrounding the earth. *This* was the transformation of the physical substances.

Christ died for us, but *we* also died for Him.

In the moment that the drops of His blood touched the earth the consciousness of humans descended into their "etheric bodies" and beheld for a short duration of time the greatest event the earth was ever permitted to experience. Upon returning to their physical bodies they all had become knowing to a high degree. They felt it first as a strong inner experience; it changed later to an unconscious sentiment of awe and magnificence. This feeling gradually weakened with the passing of the centuries, but the power of the inner voice remained as a nucleus that rests in *everyone,* becoming especially vocal in times of distress.

This inner core has become much stronger in every human being since the advent of Christ than during the millennia before.

October 24, 1915

You need not be afraid that these communications with you might harm me. Naturally, I would advance faster without the direct connection with you. However, I *want* to keep it up, and my will is equal to a command from me. I have told you that with your cooperation I must fulfill an important mission. *I have received permission* to stay in communication with you as long as you follow me.—The time will come when I can no longer remain in this close connection with you. I hope you will be far enough advanced by then so as not to need my help anymore.

Christ's appearance on earth was a sacrifice of the highest order because nothing of its kind has transpired since the creation of this earth. The whole of mankind is *still* living *entirely* under the influence of this mighty event.

God's Son has united Himself with humanity and will only be redeemed from these bonds when humanity will not need *Him* any longer and shall set *Him* free.

Then will His work be finished, and God's justice will rule

also on earth, because everyone will have understood Christ's sacrifice and will then tread the blessed path of perfection.

I want to tell you something today; please take it really to your heart: observe the hours of prayer! When you begin the new day, let your soul ascend to the Father of Light, and pray. You will gain the spiritual and physical strength for the whole day that way. The hours for spiritual devotion should be set at regular times so the spirit may then turn completely to daily tasks and fulfill them efficiently. Planned division and method between physical and spiritual occupations are essential.

October 25, 1915

I held my wings over you with the blessings of love, protecting and thanking you.

You were in the temple of consecration at a time when great calm and peace of nature abide devoutly at its portals, and you looked in at the wonderful work your love's world of thought has created for me. Few sanctuaries of this kind, which spread forces of blessing, exist. It has been built beautifully and solemnly by your loving hands.—Beaming with happiness I await you on the path of your approach—and lead you to see the novelty of birth of each new day. As you leave I accompany you out of my sanctified halls and plead for God's blessing for you, my beloved ones! With this token of love you wander then among men and tend to your duties in the spirit of devotion and surrender to God's will, Who created you and had sent you forth.

So you continue on your way strengthened; in you the

currents of my love pulsate; around you the world of
sublime thoughts, and the assemblage of figures of light
who originate in the regions to which you ascend to me.
Go in peace!

When, in the evening before you fall asleep, you have the
ardent wish to meet me, then it will surely come to pass.
But you must think of it intensively and pray for it before
sleep overtakes you.

You shall have some memory on awakening, and as the
astral body returns into the physical body you will carry
the images correctly into day consciousness. This experience signifies remembered pictures of the astral world in
which the astral body (the soul) abides during sleep.

I beg you fervently to arrange for the possibility of
working undisturbed for one or two hours because it is a
trying experience for us if we must withdraw suddenly just
as the stream begins to flow. I understand this may be
difficult for you, but your will to succeed is strong enough.

> Empower the wings to holy flight,
> Steel your heart for eternal courage.
> Go to battle and fight for the good—
> Remain victorious despite death and blood!

October 26, 1915

I abide among you with the sun in my heart. The warm
rays penetrate you and endow you with peace. You were
victorious over your lives, over death, because a holy

power proceeds from the overcoming of earthly affairs; it lightens your wings of spiritual cognition.

The last important decision was rendered today when my brother entered the place of my final rest. He was strong and I could approach him without the pain of mourning piercing his heart like a spear.—My higher ego—my Self—enfolded him as a cloud of love and peace. Moments of anxiety shall no longer vex me; no permanent separation will ever part us. This was the final test for me; *You* have passed it and therefore *I have become* free! I close my eyes humbly in gratitude for the fulfillment of my wishes, which were yours also.

You will be seeking for me in those high realms of light from now on;—there, in the vast halls of peace, which you will enter with understanding presentiments whenever you are thinking of me at the place of consecration. "Glory to You, eternal God, we thank You, Oh Almighty, Who gave us peace through His eternal Love.

"Grace! Holy dawn of fulfillment! Your Holiness is reflecting its splendor even unto us. Your Spirit, radiantly illumined, penetrates the All—and we surrender our hearts in humility. Amen."

I am yours from now on, always and eternally; Sigwart.

October 31, 1915

The greater our advancement in spiritual development, the wider will become the circle of human beings to whom we can give our love. We do not love one being only in the world! Thus arises the wonderful harmony that then sounds as a perfectly sounding chord. Each note will chime by itself, but in harmony lies beauty.

Oh, God, Who wills to redeem me,
For Your love's sake I must follow You.
Show me the way
And I'll tread in Your footsteps,
Because Jesus Christ, Your Son,
Patiently leads me on the path of redemption.
Death He has suffered for me,
And the young dawn blossoms for us.

November 1, 1915

The strings sound brightly, but you do not hear them because you cannot react to these vibrations. We, who are gathering around you, hear this gentle, pure music. You are deaf and blind to everything about you however. Yet, be patient and practice your spiritual exercises until one day your eyes will be opened. All gifts have to be asked for; we, too, pray for them. Through supplication only shall our wishes be granted. You still believe everything happens by itself. *Nothing* comes of itself, not with you, nor with us.

Winged and unwinged souls are criss-crossing this place. Winged are we who have freed ourselves from the chaotic gray masses, and we behold the sun-arrayed summit of the holy mountain. Everything is a great becoming—nothing is at a standstill. But a spark of divinity, hidden within us, must light up in order to enable us to grip helpfully the spokes of the wheel of progress. This spark is the impetus for soaring upward, because *in it* lies the longing for unity with the primeval shores that it had left behind;—*in it* lies the will to return, great and strong, to the community from whose grasp it had slipped, as a wish slips from our lips, to return as a deed fulfilled to gladden us.

In this spark weaves the power that received its life through the breath of God. *It* creates a new being through God's nearness, and—liberating itself in time—develops individually. This spark, raised up by the desire to rejoin again the heavenly fields, and being carried by the rays of light and warmth, which the primeval Spirit had emitted as threads of love, *it* lights up with its divine power the garments in whose protection *it* is able to finish its work of development.

We also wander this way and are being separated more and more from the earth-bound ones, who would find the path only if they seek for it with the eyes of humility and would willingly fold their hands in prayer.

Three tree-tops reach with their crowns into the etheric blue,
Three roads lead to their sun-lit tips;
The path of love or surrender.
The path of faith or humility.
The path of suffering or renunciation.

You may choose freely the one path whose forces you deem akin to your own:
Many walk the thorn-strewn path of love over hills and dales.
Some choose the broad, much intertwined road of faith. Few are those who walk the way of pain and renunciation. Its steep, narrow path rises up straight. These lonely souls climb speedily upward, unmindful of the towering cliffs to the right, and the abyss to the left, carried by the power that results from the will to overcome. They have

outgrown the lower self, the earthly sheaths, which served them as vehicles to victory.

You, too, are going various ways, yet *all of you* are ascending. Fulfillment is awaiting you above!

Look up to the summit's highest peak.

There, embedded in clouds, bathed in light, rises in majesty of greatness and power, *The Temple of Consecration.*

Enter, and your souls will tremble before the spirit's divine power of recognition.

November 2, 1915
All Souls' Day

All the bells pealed today and humans on earth paid tribute to their dead. Not you, because you know I am not dead.

How terribly the word rings in my ears. What does it mean "to die," "to vanish?"—Have I disappeared? Luckily you use that word seldom; it would be the destruction of your power. Did you not feel yourselves how untrue the word is as it escapes your lips? First, you speak of "having died," in the next moment you hear and sense me! How fortunate for us to have overcome what people call "to die."

True, something has perished that I had possessed, but of what importance is that compared with my real "I"? My physical existence was of the shortest duration relative to eternity. How quickly the physical body has disintegrated through your self-denial and strength, all to my benefit. As long as one lives on earth, however, one must be concerned with the physical body. Great Masters have

61

loved and fostered their bodies as worthy vehicles for the higher spirit. Therefore it is the duty of man to care for his physical body, for if it is ill, ugly and frail the spirit feels unhappy in it and the span of life he has to complete becomes too long for him and a torment. In order to feel well and comfortable the spirit must nurture its body accordingly. But to wallow in sensual indulgence for the sake of enjoying the body is *wrong*. Take care of yourself in such a way that the spirit is satisfied with its garment. The soul of man is delicate and tender. It reacts to every thought and thereby changes its color. A soul is harmed easily. Even a thought of disgust injures the gentle web. Therefore you will understand well how pleasing human beings are who only harbor joy, hope, love and the sun within themselves.

November 4, 1915

I suffered in the beginning because of you. Too many ties held me back, would not let me go, bonds of love! These I had to transform into other feelings, and because you did the same, the bond was forged for all eternity. Nothing can separate us anymore, neither life nor death.
Our love is eternal!

Sister, you felt tonight my agonies of the early period. There was an unending loneliness without you. *All* of you who had been close to me were left behind. Then I found new friends here with whom I now feel happy and content. But *I* was *alone* because I had been attached to you with all my life's forces; for this reason my departure was such pain. But I do not suffer anymore, you may believe that.

62

I can hardly imagine a life on earth with you now in my physical body; I would not exchange my present existence for it. If God Almighty would say to me, "By returning to your discarded earthly sheaths you may return to your loved ones," I would answer, "No, Lord, I am free. I have everything my heart desires. I have my loved ones even *more so* than before, and here I am experiencing glory and eternity."

I give you words of consolation:
"My child, I would help you in your great empty solitude, in your eternal pain, in your strong longing for the sublime, and in your love for Me.
Come to Me, oh come! I would gladly give you My helping hand, you poor lonely child of man. Yet your longing lacks wings. But time will heal your suffering. I may not draw you up to Me, up to the holy summits of eternity. *Alone* you must be, *alone* you must strive for everlasting bliss. Then your wings will grow and in all-forgiving blissful flight you will come to Me.
Turn back your gaze once more at the threshold of eternity to the island of lasting pain. Never again will you be lonesome, because by your *own* power you have lifted yourself to the heights of glory, to Me, the Ruler of Eternity."
You see, *you yourselves* must rise, then will you have fulfilled the greatest task on earth—overcoming death.

November 8, 1915

Sorrow, sadness and grief are vestments that hug you tightly and oppress you with their embrace. They feel as

63

though they are part of you and rob you of life and
strength; the lustre of your eyes is dimmed by their veils.
You see the shining light of the sun no more, nor the
sparkle of the stars. You have become a world of pain,
locked out of the bliss-bestowing nature of God.—Break
your fetters! Rise to the freedom of *will*.
The broken shell will lie at your feet and you shall breathe
blissfully—liberation!

Great days are beginning for me now.
The symphonic composition will be performed for the
benefit of mankind and for the highest bliss of all of us.
G. (a war comrade), the good fellow will also attend. He
came to me at last. It took him a long time; he steadily
refused to be sensible and acknowledge that he was devoid
of a physical body. All talk was useless; I finally left him
alone. But today he came happily to me. I was truly glad;
he will come to me often now.
I called together all the others who are close to me so that
they may also feel lifted by the work. My thoughts will be
with you especially, my dear ones, as it will be only half
the joy without you.
The partition of the work is fundamentally different from
performances on earth. First come the notes in their
sequence, then one constructs the chords by oneself, and
then the harmony sounds out of thousands of spiritual
beings, who give it various changes and dimensions
according to the power of each individual being.
The great songs will follow, many of which I have
composed. Songs without words, sung without a larynx,
yet with the perfection of sublime experience.
I can hardly tell you what this means. Imagine, for
instance, that a thousand glamorous tenors sing one and

the same song, and this chorus sounds in its most various sublimations from the highest mountains into the quiet valleys. This may give you an approximate idea of the experience.

Then thoughts, emotions, tones and colors blend together as a finality, divide into groups again, which simultaneously emit their art and power with such force that the heavenly spheres and parts of the earth tremble to their foundations.

These performances last several days by terrestrial time. I am happy I also was able to compose part of the creation. Only those who possess the capacity and talent may give birth to such works, as is also customary on earth. I had been commissioned to do a large part of the composition with two other souls, and even now I shall have to work hard at the performances.

The preparations begin today, but that is not the beginning by far. I shall tell you as soon as the performances commence.

. . . You see, my dear Sister, your feelings for everything that concerns me are lifting you up as on wings to the luminous heights of eternal truth.

Truth is the key note in everything. Unfortunately it is being veiled from all sublimity on earth by thick layers of untruth and calumny. But you have strong wings with hidden powers for reaching up to the highest.

> Father, God of eternity!
> Our souls are aglow with love for you!
> And we are kneeling here,
> Repentance within us,
> And the wish in our hearts,

Our soul afire
With a devotional spirit,
Thrice be love,
Thrice be bliss,
Thrice be the Trinity,
Life and salvation!
Amen—Amen and Amen.

Pray to the Trinity who harbors the profoundest depths within itself. Your surrounding will be shaken by the sense and sound, thus everything undesirable will be kept at a distance.
Say this mantram often aloud, alone and together.

November 10, 1915

Let go of your doubts and brooding—it hinders your flight. After you have raised yourselves above the depressing miasma of your earth you will be able to comprehend what would be today a vain attempt of understanding for you.
Have confidence—it is I, your Brother, who is guiding you. Do not seek for explanations, but harken to the echo within you, which will reveal everything true and sublime in you. When you have found that echo, then bow your head in humility before the incomprehensible.
I have gone ahead of you and am smoothing the way for you.
My hands are blessing you in hours of worry. I pray for you in hours of doubt.
I help you also with my love whenever you seem to

stumble, and I am leading you on to eternity, toward peace.

Our Father is waiting!—A wreath is being woven from the blossoms of your prayers and your love, to embellish the portals of eternity when the way to glory shall be opened for you.

November 11, 1915

You are the strings of my lute, I pluck a different note with each one, and the sound waves are rising up in beautiful, quiet streams to the spheres above you. There they fill our halls with clear pure themes and merge with our songs to a magnificent edifice of power.

I am playing your strings through the strength of my love, and your notes ascend on the waves of eternal love and longing!—I am the player,—I can create great works through you. I need you, everyone of you, my dear ones, because the clear voices of your souls are the forces that are building up my works.—You should become a splendid chorus, and the waves of your songs should lap against the stairway leading to the heavenly spheres.

I need you, the pealing chimes of your spiritual ascension. Let yourselves be led by changing harmonies and chords, thereby transcending dissonances that are await-ing dissolution.—Abide!

The great sound, in which all tunes are combined in heavenly harmonies, *shall* ring and will fill you with profound rapture. But the time is not yet.

Practice!

So everyone may have the strength to swing upward in

songs.—Then I shall take you, you wonderful tones of my lute, gratefully to Him, the Highest! A singer who shall sing his best of songs to *Him.*

Consecrate the notes of your souls to me so I may change them into *heavenly* timbre, which will bestow wings for the flight to eternity.

The music performances have just begun. I am completely enthralled by the experience. It is impossible to describe it. I would never have thought I could comprehend nearly all of the meaning. Most everyone knows how to listen, but few are those who understand.

I was permitted to call you too, your highest ego only,—the I you hardly know, yet it is the core of your whole being.

The premonition I had felt on earth had to do with this sublime spiritual experience. This premonition has been fulfilled now. The clearest essence of these spiritual harmonies will penetrate the earthly spheres and should influence mankind. Much illness will be healed, pains of soul will be relieved, and good seeds will be encouraged to germinate and sprout.

The time flies;—I must return, I am expected, they are calling the creator of the three songs of the spheres. The name by which I am called is difficult to put into words; it means something like "the uncovering of the sun,"—many of the spiritual beings know me by this name. Not all of them, because the undeveloped ones here also fail to recognize the more advanced ones. The performances continue. I have learned much from them. They will begin to ebb away gradually by tomorrow, but this will last a long time, as it is a slow fading away and exhalation of music and sentiments.

God be with you; I am ever more closely united with you the more *you* work on yourselves.

I am with you, I, your brother.

November 15, 1915

The performances have ended. A roundalay by a community of the most radiant spiritual beings was the finale. They all had to float in groups through space as the crowning of the greatest event ever. Everyone has dispersed now and I am coming to you to tell you my impressions.

Is there anything, my dear ones, that can compare with this?—No, we are all but poor children of men, I as well as you. This I had to recognize, because the loftiest spiritual beings were present at this event. Very few could see them because here, too, these sublime beings remain hidden from the less developed souls. I was able to catch a short glimpse through a kind of mist, and this proved to be the culmination of these magnificent hours. One feels then the reality of Divinity, of Whom we hear so much here and to Whom our longing and prayers ascend. It was a moment of the most powerful sentiments I have ever experienced. You have contributed to this possibility by fostering and easing my spiritual development. Without your help I perhaps would not have been permitted to participate. You see how your surroundings are blossoming and bearing fruit.

How your various walks of life are illuminated! Whatever used to be dim and beset with obstacles has now become bright, clear and open.—You have stepped beyond your foreordained karma. You have created a new one for yourselves by the power of love.

It shall become still lighter around you, believe me, your brother, who has foregone his physical body for you, for his country, for humanity, and for himself.

I must return to my friends whom I left in order to tell you of the completion of our work. They are waiting for me to exchange thoughts concerning the wonderful happenings. This is the same as with you on earth. You also converse with your friends after you have heard something beautiful.

November 16, 1915

. . . No remorse—but have the will to do better, and sublimate this resolution into deeds. When you concentrate your thoughts daily on the same subject and at the same time, you are not only creating spiritual strength but you are also molding your character. To forget the hour of devotion—as you did today—is harmful because a link is missing in the chain. But if such negligence reenforces the resolution to do better in the future, and one follows it up, then the harm becomes beneficial. Learn to *will,* and subordinate your whole being to this will, then you shall become master of yourself.—Practice, and practice again!

> Dream,—
> You wandering soul
> Slowly you glide through the night.
> Just once let my eye see
> The primeval force of all being.
> In quiet nights I prayed to You—

Always groping, seeking, longing—
Give me understanding to brighten the night.
Let me awake in the joy of cognition!
My all I shall give to You—my God,
To live through one night only
Deeply and *knowingly.*—
Above the tips of the trees hovers the moon,
Above the sea's glitter sparkles a star.
All is primeval power and eternity.
For one night only, oh God,
Let me be steeped in wisdom—
I beg of You!

November 18, 1915

"At the Place of Consecration."
All thoughts united here have the power to carry you to me.
Deepest wisdom is resting within it and eternity is hidden in its lap.
You all came with profound thoughts; you have supported me with this power. How great was the hour you have spent here! Peace is spreading far and wide, emanating from this Place of Consecration, which is lighting up like a sun.

November 19, 1915

What grace! The final act has been consummated now. How fortunate, the blessing of the earthly body has been fulfilled! I felt for a moment, through you, the pain of

71

severance. These earthly remnants still made their demands on me. But now I have said farewell *forever* to my old garment. The pain made my spirit tremble for a moment, but then I was free. Now I am relieved, and my earthly shell has also begun its eternal sleep, which will end with its dissolution.

You have helped me to lead the body to its final rest at last, you have taken the strength of self-sustenance from it, you have destroyed its desire for survival. I had to make the test today because the time had come when I had to separate myself from it *forever;* there I recognized your help.—I believe you have no idea how much you have done.

I was allowed to bless my body, because it was ready for disintegration.

I want to say the following for your understanding: We all separate from our earthly sheath, it becomes foreign to us, and we lose all connection with it. But then comes the moment when we must gaze on the material world for the last time before the final decay of these remnants.

Everyone descends to his once-worn raiment and will observe whether the innumerable thoughts of the bereaved have done their good or bad work on it.

Thoughts can sustain a body!

It is self-understood that this last visit with the old long-forgotten body engenders memories of the life on earth, but only for a brief moment.

I was separated from my body soon after death. I did not know it anymore. But *everyone* has to experience what I have gone through there. It is similar to a fleeting reunion with someone we have not seen since childhood and had therefore almost forgotten.

Later: I have sensed everything that you, my Brother, had to criticize about my information. You see, I told you something that has a positive connotation for my spirit, but a negative one for your brains.

These are problems that cannot be conveyed in the logical fashion of humans. It is deeper than what you can comprehend.

All this has nothing to do with physical connections, nor with spiritual threads that remain. These are rather waves that emanate from there and have to be intercepted once more—an essence of experiences that persisted, but that has been destroyed now. If a body is cremated or destroyed in some other way, this essence—if we may call it thus—remains also. It stays at the place of the sudden transformation, and the spirit returns once more in order to control the surviving essence, because it originated from that spirit. It is nothing physical, nor is it connected directly with the body, but it can be aroused through many grieving thoughts of the ones left behind.

I saw, or rather sensed my earthly body again for the first time at that opportunity,—but now the place beneath the oak tree is empty again as before. Above it arches the dome of the magnificent temple of peace, built by you, my dear ones.

Sigwart.

November 20, 1915

Life on earth is not one of joy, it is harsh and burdensome. Everyone feels this, and yet, how many cling fast to this earth. I was permitted to tell you much, therefore the thought of leaving the physical body behind should cause

73

no more feelings of shudder or regret. Life on earth is bearable only if one considers it a brief period of transition. No worry has importance, and none we should subscribe to it.

You may compare the event of incarnation with an unpleasant journey you must accomplish. At the destination—on earth—you will feel as though shut into a courtyard surrounded by high walls. You can see the sky above you, but you are convinced that it is unattainable. There you stay until you are called back again.

A few of you, however, can surmount the walls by your spiritual development. The confinement will no longer exist for those because they possess the freedom of the spirit.

You should get thus far, then sorrow and worry will transform into bliss.

I pity you sometimes when I have to observe your little worries because they are really *little* worries. Great sorrows are only those that concern the soul, when soul or spirit are harmed; when doubting man is angry with his God because He does not scatter roses on man's path, *these* are great worries for us!

Remember that, all of you, who feel embraced by sorrow. Remember and remain strong; you must rise above these worries. God is with you always, and provides what He considers best for you and your development.

November 21, 1915

I have been with you in the church. I sensed through you what I used to feel there.

The Passion of Christ that was read caused remarkable waves. I was immersed deeply in devotion—not because I was moved by the pastor's sermon, but a second service was being celebrated parallel to yours, far loftier and sublime. I listened to its magnificent message. The song you heard was continued by us. How beautiful was the atmosphere. A holy blessing emanated from the light-filled heights and crowned this hour. I received it in humility, and the power penetrated to you also.

Whatever you sense as sentiments and *feelings,* however dimly, is for us an *experience.* How rich I am to be able to divine more than is generally possible for us here, as only *these* sentiments are important here.

Your spiritual experiences, which can be compared only with dim, vague emotions, will be changed later to strong, consciously experienced realities.

I am able to sense all of you even when you are separated; I divide myself then and am present in various places at the same time. I acquired this capacity only recently.

I came to you during the devotion.

Our Father is magnanimous because he has received me into His arms. I came to Him, injured as I was for my Homeland's sake. He spoke to me thus: "Here you are, my son Sigwart, come to Me and rest from the pains of your wounds, which you desired to suffer for your country." I then reclined gently in His arms: "Father, You my dear Father, is it alright so?" I said to Him.

"My son, you died a death of sacrifice, the most glorious of all deaths. Is your wish fulfilled now, your ardent wish, my son?"

75

"Yes, my dear Father!—My wish was more fervent than my love for life."

Thus, I stepped across the threshold still aglow from the love to this longed for wish. I had known even before I took on the new earthly body that the Father had granted my request to die for my homeland. *It meant heavenly grace for me.*—I had to tell you, this was my wish, so you may feel it deeply in your hearts.

Close your eyes and pray for the warrior Sigwart, who has exchanged his armor for the white cloak of peace.

My battles are over, but my songs are chiming and floating through your environment.

I feel how my song has moved you. All my endeavors on earth were aimed at this death of sacrifice. Christ was my hero. How often I had serenaded Him! As a youth I had harbored the vague desire in my heart to become a hero.—But then I was immersed in art, but the deeds of a hero wafted through it even then. What a shining example was the "Song of the Iliad" for me. How I was fired by the enthusiasm for these heroes. Then the great conflagration broke loose on earth: War, war everywhere!—My country was in danger.—There and then it lit up in me that now I might become a hero, a hero of deeds at last.

"Sigwart, Sigwart, where is your sword?"

I heard the call, I had to follow. Was it not the ancient call?

"Sieg, Sieg!" (victory) I was named. So I heard it within me.

"Yes, I *Sigwart,* await victory." (*WARTe des SIEGes*)

Then I fell, wounded, a feeling of bliss in my heart.—Thus I gave my life for you, my dear homeland! And there above was written: "Welcome, welcome, Sigwart, who has remained true to his name."

You see, thus I died, such were the last great days of my life. I had to tell you how deeply my soul was immersed in it all in those days.

November 22, 1915

Holy! Holy! Holy!
Do you feel the hour's solemnity?
Around you a shining circle
Of spirits are gathering
Who fervently implore
The Godhead's blessing,
And heavenly grace,
Your soul to immerse
In Divine strength.
Bow—bow down,
So matter may perish,
And with it sin—
The oppressing heritage.
The earth's dark clod is your grave—
Yet above is *life*
And eternal bliss.

In the gleam of liberation
Your soul is aglow,
Awakening it expands
For the heavenly flight,
And slowly it begins to soar.—
Spread—broaden—lift

Your white wings.
Swing—sing—sound.
Longing will carry you joyously
Up to the luminous home!

November 24, 1915

Today was a practice hour, we were allowed to test our strength in order to see to what extent it would suffice. Ordinarily such attempts are controlled from higher up. It was a joy for me to work all by myself. However, we are not permitted as yet to experiment with our self-gained power. It means more practice for now until we shall be left to ourselves, but this will not happen until much later. There was a kind of demonstration before the Masters today. It was a great joy to be able to show our accomplishments at last. This had to do with thought forces; we had to extinguish thoughts and then recreate them. We had to bring new beings to life with our will power, and to free ourselves from any external influences and currents. Through feelings we had to call forth colors that changed their shades according to their delicacy. It was an hour of real instruction under the supervision of the highest Masters.

These occupations went hand in hand with my music and with my spiritual connection with you, which also took time and effort. I have not wasted a minute in idleness. The mountains I still have to climb lie before me, bright and clear in purest sunlight, without danger, without obstacles. Seeing the goal before me as beautiful and distinct is an exhilarating experience. Therefore, you, too, must work on yourselves with all the energy of your will power.

We shall never completely comprehend the spiritual essence as long as we remain connected with our physical bodies, no matter how voluminous the research we carry on.

The unquestioning confidence and matter-of-course attitude with which you accept and understand whatever I convey to you is the valuable thread that runs through our present intercourse. As a consequence, my own development is an unusual and exceptional one; for this reason you are unable to explain to yourselves certain phenomena. You have played an important role in helping me to divest myself of greeds—as they are called—because through your comprehension of spiritual things, and your cooperation such desires have not been attracted by earthly sentiments. Thank God, I myself had no great material passions during my lifetime. But worldly sorrowing on your part would have sustained certain physical capacities in me that would have aroused or maintained some wishes. You have lightened my present condition through your spiritual striving in such a way that you would consider it hardly possible.

This is what I have to say to you again: I was able to divest myself of the various sheaths in peace because you did not hold me back, and *therefore we could stay together.* No matter how far I shall develop myself I shall be with you until you leave your bodies behind. But I must expect you to continue your spiritual striving in this way, then our work shall remain a mutual one.

I am entwined with you as intimately as a vine of ivy with a column of white marble.

The importance of our circle should not be underestimated. Please remain more quiet during the hour of spiritual occupation, exchange your opinions peacefully, control your thoughts in this hour especially, speak only of profound things or of spiritual questions. If you observe these rules consistently then sublime beings can always be around you. Just think: "We have been purified by God's grace, and to be worthy of it we shall sacrifice this hour for spiritual devotion."

November 27, 1915

I want to proclaim to you the majestic figure of our Saviour *Christ Jesus,* who came to you, to the poor, sin-burdened earth, by *His Own Will.* He is still living in the glory of the highest Godliness, but He is sad, because He has compassion for you, the humanity on the "earth of horror,"—as it is now called here. *He,* in His luminous heights, has heard of the creation of music, the work of sanctity. We knew not that He was present also. But I feel the after-glow now, for His might is too powerful for us not to be made aware of His blessing. It became known to me today, and this filled me with indescribable joy and deepest thankfulness.

Kneel down with me in spirit and let us thank Him for this grace out of the deepest recesses of our souls. Exalted chiming is ringing in me as a result of this holy event. I am experiencing it continuously and can enwrap myself in the

current of love that emanated from Him, the Redeemer.—
He was present, my compositions have touched His divine
spirit!
I cannot write any more today,—I was affected too deeply.
Let me rest in quiet thankfulness and let me relive the
happiness once more.

> We thank You, Father of Light,
> Together we pray to Your Highest Divinity.
> We bow down in humility,
> Because we cannot fathom Your Grace.
> In love we embrace the ray
> That emanates from You and returns to You.
> Our thoughts flow to You as subtly
> As the quiver of a dew-fresh rose leaf.
> Wings carry us—yes, *our*
> Spirit, all the way up to You.
> They bring greetings to You of poor men,
> Who are rich in faith,
> Yet poor in wisdom.
> Healing,
> Blessing,
> Heavenly unity,
> We thank you!
> Help, holiest Power!
> *Yours,*
> *Mine,*
> *Eternally.*

November 29, 1915

A tender thread unites human beings whose souls are
intimately close to one another. This thread will become

81

so strong with time that the connection will continue even later between the living and the departed ones. Such a unity is always of the greatest importance and power whenever a circle of people is forged whose thinking and feeling, and also desires are of a similar kind.

How easy your dying will be if you continue to strive spiritually as you did during these past months. Then all shall be simple. I shudder whenever I think of those souls without faith who are called away from the earth. This is the worst that can happen.

As I was hovering in the regions of sensations I met an old man who seemed familiar to me. I was amazed to meet him there. What might he be doing here? He said to me: "You see, my brother, I am an old man and really did not need to return to this region, but I have forgotten something on earth. There are remnants I must look for here, for I must collect them. This job is not easy and it is disagreeable. It is the result of one being called away from the earth without having organized one's spiritual fruits and experiences, which must be in such order and readiness that we can return without having to come back to these regions, I had overcome long ago."

He was grateful to me for helping him with the task, and I believe he will be finished with it soon.

This tale will be difficult for you to understand, but I cannot word it differently. Perhaps you will sense the meaning of it. I was allowed to pass this occurrence on to you as a help to your further course of life. You will have to fathom the significance of it, each in his own way.

December 4, 1915

You dear ones are making life so difficult for yourselves! Is it really impossible for you to free your spirits from the earthly burdens and worries?—It is not easy for us who exist in the spiritual world to remain in such a tormenting turmoil. All these restless currents, akin to a stormy raging sea, are penetrating to us. This is terrible as you are swallowed up completely in it and I cannot find you then. We can stay with you and can influence you only when harmony and quietness of soul surround you.

December 6, 1915

. . . You will be able to develop yourself even while attending to daily duties, do not despair therefore, everything will come as it must!
Have faith in God and believe in my fidelity.

December 7, 1915

(We submitted the messages to Rudolf Steiner, the most important investigator of supersensible worlds in our time. He kept them for several weeks and scrutinized the communications seriously, being also conscious of the responsibility involved. He proclaimed them to be fully authentic and of an unusually high standard. He was so interested that he asked to be kept informed.)

How glad I am!—Had you expected a different result? I hope our connection is proven for good now, for outsiders, too. I understand fully why you wanted to resort to the means of a definite proof. I would have done the same in your position. We shall work now so that certainty shall ripen in yourselves also.

You shall see how much will yet result from our work. I can feel your happiness, and that makes me also glad.

The time will come when people will have developed their spiritual organs and will be able to communicate with their dear departed ones,—but humans are not that far developed at present.

Such communications will appear as dream images at first, but they are more because these clear dream pictures are founded on truth.

All this shall come when the time is ripe for it. God's clock does not stop, and its gears never wear out. Thus, let us wait in humility until His clock strikes the hour of the overcoming of death, and let us thank our Father for the wishes already fulfilled.

(As an answer to a question)
. . . Even after death we cannot immediately see *higher* beings, but only after one has removed all of one's sheaths.

December 9, 1915

All your thoughts that are penetrating to me now are being controlled from higher up because it will be decided whether or not I shall be permitted to continue this unusual communication with you. The decision does not rest with me. I can tell you about it definitely in a few days. This was debated today. Two Masters discussed it and then they came to me. My life is simpler now without great events. I work much, but I am not allowed to think of my music because it would divert me from my other tasks. I am much alone and meditate. I have evolved an exact plan for our further mutual activities. I think we should start from the beginning with the very first rules for acquiring supersensible capacities. It is senseless to try to accomplish something imperfect in this regard. I want you to develop far enough to lessen the differences in our forms of existence, thus to be able to sense and see through everything, depending on the extent of your development. You must think your thoughts in exact sequences during the day. The uncontrolled whirring about of your thoughts has to end. I have pupils here, too, but naturally I am more concerned about you. I was afraid at first that this wonderful task would be taken away from me. Control your thoughts *very much* these days so the Masters will let me keep this happiness.

December 11, 1915

The Masters have decided,—I may go on speaking to you. I was afraid I might still experience some disappointment because you were not free in your world of thoughts concerning me during these past days. But the Masters have tested *everything,* not only the last unfavorable days, as I had feared. Thus they saw the immense power you have created because all has remained of what you have done so far. The uncertainty is past, we can begin with our work now.

85

(Not having been aware of the message above, a sister residing in another country received the following confirmation a few hours later.)

M., my Sister!
I may continue to speak to you all!—You have won, and we may begin with our mutual task. How happy I am over this fortunate certainty. I know you will be glad, for this reason I came to tell you also of this decision.

You should concentrate on these prayers:

Morning:

I shall dedicate this day to You, my Redeemer. Nothing should reach me that is not emanating from You. Great is my will, Oh God, but greater yet my love for You.

Forenoon:

> I am and You in me.
> I was and You by me.
> I will and You are mine.

Noontime:

> I have the will to reach for the Highest.
> I shall attain it.
> You must forgive me,
> I have sinned

And am still sinning.
But now I know You are coming to me
Therefore the sin is leaving me.
Help me, Exalted One, Almighty!
Your will is my will,
I bow down before You.

Afternoon:

Godhead of the world,
You are Strength, Love and Eternity,
In You we should abide.
It all repeats itself,
Eternal turning of evolution's wheel,
Until our path of sorrow
Will end in the sea of Light.
Only then may I rest
After the day's fulfillment—
In You.

To a Mother:

Your child is smothering in a thick layer of thoughts begot
of fear and worry. I could not reach him at first as these
are wrapped around him, layer upon layer. All that must
go because it is as impure and heavy as a thick mass in our
sight. The poor child, only with great effort can he unfold
in it. You must keep him in purer fluids, which emanate
from you and surround him. He can be helped only if you
overcome your anxiety and treat him as a healthy,
life-enjoying strong child.

Every single loving thought of the parents penetrates the child, therefore do not forget you can help him only by your own development. It will be different later on, but the most important time is until the seventh year.

I have perceived what you said and I shall answer you. My messages are revelations for you, the holiest you could obtain through your love, which has raised you to the spheres that are making our intercourse possible. Now I want to lead you and lift you with me out of the dross of earthly burdens. You should learn to breathe, and to behold freely as much as you are allowed to. It is my wish to exalt you, to cause the germination of the seeds that are lying in you, and to show you how to bring to fruition your innermost treasures.

The fetters of earthly life are still known to me, and because I am still able to feel my humanness, I pity you, and want to show you the way out of this encumbrance. It is *your* free will to follow my call. Everyone will feel inwardly what is right. Be never afraid I might draw you away from your duties,—*no*—you should become stronger, more capable, so you can confront them as masters and not as knaves. You should feel how much you can still grow, how much your surroundings can sprout and blossom when you raise your spirit regularly and teach it to master your body.

We know how far each one of you could advance, and we mourn when we see the fertile fields approach the summer untilled. Therefore I want to help you to attain the fortune I am enjoying in freedom, and that is within your reach while still on earth. If you develop yourselves, then your actions will be fired and lit up from within, and this will enhance your strength for attending to your duties, which are also sacred to me.

You are surely not living on earth in order to remain immersed in matter and to search *there* for your area of duties. This will lift itself to the degree you yourselves will rise, and learn to survey:—what you are to do,—what is your calling,—what you are to live for. The power for fulfilling your duties always comes from above, and by immersing yourselves in the higher spheres you will learn how to fulfill the tasks according to the Creator's will.

Judge, act, and fulfill while standing over and above it all.

You must see it as a grace that I am permitted to tell you all this, as it signifies an easing of your earthly existence. Otherwise, you are destined to wander through it, straining for liberation all by yourselves. But promise to follow my directions only when your strength is up to it,—lest it may harm you.

Never forget, the temple of God that you represent may be shaken violently or destroyed by an inadvertent untruth, and become deeply cracked as by the effects of an earthquake. Control not only your thoughts, but also your words. The power for your exaltation depends on your inner disposition and on the purity of your way of life, hold fast to these.

December 16, 1915

An important festival is taking place today but we are allowed to be present in thought only; we shall hear afterwards about the holy event. The highest Masters will attend. It is a festival of the most exalted Divinities. All Mysteries from primeval times to the present will be re-enacted, embracing eons of years. All of this will be a combined celebration of the truest and purest rituals that were performed in the Mysteries.

All the holy festivals that had been celebrated and experienced since the beginning of earthly evolution will be enacted by the Masters as the holiest of events. Only the smaller part of every mystical or religious festival is really *true* and great, and *these* parts only shall be combined and used for you and the world. The high degree of holiest sentiments and self-control contained therein represents an immense power, impossible to describe with words.

I believe the decision is near whether humanity will have rest for awhile, or whether the raging of the elements should continue. Are these holy and exalted currents strong enough to overcome the weapons and the wild elements?—I do not know. I have heard of all this through a high mediator who, albeit, was not present there. I was permitted to convey to you, however, the few things I have been told. It is the most important news, nevertheless; consider it a great gift therefore.

M., my Sister, I want to thank you for having listened to me. You also have prepared a place for me in your heart; it is luminous in its purity. Your love, which carries you up to me, was the power that allowed me to come to you.

You gave me the possibility, through these waves that are akin to mine, to unite myself completely with your soul and make me able to speak to you. Thank the exalted One in the light-filled heights, not me, for showing you how to become a home for my thoughts.

Your Sigwart.

December 17, 1915

The great assignment I had to accomplish here is finished, —now I am *free.* I may choose whether or not I want to continue to work in the same direction, i.e., if I want to acquire more forces and develop myself as quickly as possible, or if I want to take up again great, magnificent assignments in music. I shall choose whichever brings me nearer to you. I renounce gladly any overly fast advancement for your sake. This will be decided today. Everything has transpired according to fixed rules and laws up to now. But now I have arrived at the point where I may choose the further direction of activities. Generally this is only the case after many years, figured by your concepts of time. You can see from that how diligently I have worked lately. You have no idea how infinitely happy and grateful I am for having been permitted to initiate you as your teacher into the spiritual truths, which alone are of real value.

(His opera, which he had finished shortly before the war, had its premiere now, six months after his death.)

December 19, 1915

M., my Sister, you have asked me often if you could do something for me. I come to you now with joyful tidings.

I shall tell you what you can give me out of your free will. I received the permission to be present at the performance of my opera,—to see and to hear the effects of my work in the earthly realms. But I need a mediating link that is completely at my disposal for this purpose. Would you do that? Would you relinguish your earthly senses entirely to me for my use, so I may see and hear physically as you would? . . . (later) . . . I thank you!—I thought you would be glad that I came to you with my request. I feel it as a sacred gift, the best you could give me by granting my wish. I thank you in every way that we are able to give thanks from this sphere.

Your Sigwart.

You should hear the reflection of truth, of sublimity I had creating my musical work on earth, and immerse your-selves in its depth. Even more, once your spirit has become lucid, then the holy sentiment that was woven into this composition will appear to you more beautiful.

The portals of my temple are opened wide, a sea of light is streaming out from it and binding your beings and mine into one. We are united in spirit—but you will perceive—when severed from earthly sounds, the sublimity of fulfillment contained in the work I was called upon to create.

I am more alive than ever before and can sense everything. When thoughts of sadness over my departure reappear, you can not hide them from me. My feelings are more alert in such moments because I perceive with my highest ego, while everything is veiled for you by matter. We also experience still the sensation of weeping, but only when facing moments of greatness.

I plead once more, seek for my spirit, for my real self, not for my material raiment I do not wear any more. Think of a figure of light that is akin to my earthly one.

I have my free will now and can work on whatever I enjoy. You can hardly imagine what this means here; free of the fetters of earth; free of every material worry; free of the longing for an earthly body; freed from the sorrow of the bereaved. I am indescribably fortunate. Now I can work on all the thoughts I am harboring within me.

One must steadily practice great patience here. No matter how sublime the work of art one has created, one is not allowed at first to utilize it for the benefit of others until the artist has passed all tests, and has reached a certain level of development. I wanted to tell you this so you know that one is not permitted to be active in the work of one's choice until much later. I have decided to stay with the music, my beloved music. By this decision I can remain especially close to you.

Just now I am busy with a composition. It will contain all my sublime and holy experiences of late. I shall dedicate it as a "Gift of Thanks" to my Masters who—as mediators of the Godhead—have made possible for me a life of greatness and illumination. This composition will be sung like a hymn and will be played by innumerable beings assigned to me at my disposal. You can imagine how I enjoy this work.—I shall not report to you in detail about it as I do not know myself yet how it will come out. Only the basic motive, the key, and the approximate outlines are clear to me. It is exhilarating to be able to create something big again all by myself!

I am well otherwise. I have found many dear human souls

who console me concerning my spatial separation from you. They are all amazed over my strong and intimate connection with all of you, because it is considered rare to maintain such near relationship on earth with all one's eternal friends—with all of them. But nobody is as close to me as you are.

How joyfully I look forward to the time when we shall be united here in the spiritual world! We shall mean a thousandfold more to each other than on earth, as no separation exists here.

December 24, 1915

Holy Night!

I was permitted to behold something immeasurable. I have already told you of the wonderful sounds that are streaming down into the innermost layers of the earth. But I have perceived something even more profound and much deeper than any songs. I was granted to *feel my Redeemer!* My Saviour, Christ Jesus. Waves that emanated from Him penetrated me, and I received them with the holiest cognition: Waves from *Him,* from *Him.*

I had to remain quiet, nothing was revealed to me beforehand. Then a stream of love passed by me, I knew at once: this came from God, this came from Him! But I lost consciousness in a most blessed surrender.—Why did this happen to me?—Why my strange condition?—Was I not strong enough to receive this holy stream? It came by me and wafted further on to gladden others, to bless others.

I was not mature enough, I was unable to assimilate the love, and thus it overpowered me. The stream had passed on, but a tiny heart-thought of it stayed behind, of the immensity that had flowed through the spheres and had touched me too. I shall nurture and foster this thought in my heart as one would a rare plant, which was born by love and can survive only through love. Thus I feel this heart-thought. It was the mightiest of all the events I was granted to experience.

Many beautiful and dear thoughts from you have reached me today. They came to me every so often as pretty white doves. I received each one as a gift. I have never before experienced such a lovely Christmas Eve:
It was like a receiving of all the profoundest sensations, and therefore an unspeakable joy to us leaders and teachers. For once we could surrender ourselves to the earth without fear or dread of all the cruelty that adheres to it. Generally it is no joy to approach mankind, because one is seldom rewarded with real success. It is a thankless job.—Can you comprehend how your devoted love, your striving and your understanding gladdens me?

December 24, 1915

Christmas is the holiest of festivals, because then the figure "Jesus" beheld the earth for the first time. This was the preparation for all the majestic events to come.
"Christ" *was* present there.
He Himself received the little Babe in order to assay whether it was really pure enough for His later great and difficult mission, imprisoned as He would be in matter, amidst imperfect humanity. He blessed the little child, knowing the same would become His own flesh and blood.

All the phenomena that took place at the birth of the Jesus child resulted from the lofty Spirit "Christ Jesus," who approached the child. The nature of the birth was not the miracle, *no,* the delivery was like any other, except that the mother was a perfect virgin, pure in body and spirit: but the nearness of the Son of God, the highest of all beings, caused the wondrous happenings in nature.

This is the event we celebrate: the *approach* of Christ.

You all, who have celebrated this appearance with me so often, now only do I recognize the importance of it! You are so right to be celebrating this day. We also honor it here but the date is different. Oh, this magnificent festival, this indescribable solemnity! We kneel in spirit and pray, while above the most glorious songs sound simultaneously from the regions that are unknown to us. But we may hear them today.

The whole celestial regions are permeated by them, down to the beings of the deepest spheres. These, too, are granted to sense it in their often doubting hearts. Many become believers, and for everyone of those it will also be a festival of birth, the birth of their faith.

A great part of the earth is receptive then for God.

December 25, 1915

The bells of Christmas are pealing up to us and our thoughts are united in prayer. The horizons of earth are surrounded by walls: and the waves of suffering, so colossal on earth now, all roll against these walls in a monotonous beat, and are shattered against their massiveness. This surging, heaving expanse appears like a huge terrible monster. No white caps are visible, only wave

96

after wave rising colorless to collapse again upon itself with an impotent rumble. What use the anger of human powerlessness, which lacks the impetus for comprehending the help that alone could effect the liberation from this terrible mass?

Perceive, all you poor humans, who are threatened with suffocation in the floods of unshackled elements:

The suffering is sent down as liberation from these chains. The waves of the oceans storm more powerfully against the rampart that encloses the earth; the former must tremble from this force of the surf. Shaken violently shall be its foundations.

Hail, you blessed ones, who shall see the first wave as it will gush through the breach of the wall out of the earthly prison into the regions of light!

Great will be the moment the poor earth shall experience when its waters will unite those of our heavenly spheres. Mother earth will open her eyes as if awakening from a long slumber and will behold *herself* for the first time,— her own essence the veil of sleep had hidden from her.

In the soft, blissful dawning of recognition will her God-consecrated being kneel longingly, pray, entreat and implore before the Throne of the Creator, that He may speak the Almighty word of redemption.

December 31, 1915
Sylvester

The farewell bells are ringing for the by-gone year on earth, and the mournful hearts listen apprehensively for what the new year may have in store. The period men call a year has brought much for you. You have bowed down

97

under the oppressing weight of sorrow, and your hearts have been torn by pain. But then the loving Father gave you the gift of grace and led your thoughts into the paths to your true homeland through me. Out of your tears grew the tree of true, real life,—and you understood.

Do you perceive now that you have reason to thank and not to grieve? What is separation if it means true inner joy for both parties, and if the most glorious reunion is awaiting us as God-ordained truth?

You have given me so much, you have proved your love with such strength—how much I owe you!

This old year, which I had spent in enemy territory far away, but had begun with you on earth, has turned into the greatest blessedness for me! I went ahead of you on the path we all must tread, and was granted to be more to you than I could have been on earth, and was allowed to prove to you my love by real deeds.

The Father's hands are held in blessing over you. Walk consoled and full of happy confidence across the threshold to the new year. Use it well, vow to work for your progress, on the enfoldment of your souls, and on the enlightenment of your spirit!—

These resolutions may carry you on light wings into the hour of the future. Give me your hands. Our circle encompasses not only years, not periods of time that you would try vainly to count:

"Believe and pray, say thank you and step across the earthly threshold to the altar of light beyond!"—There lies eternity, permeating our bonds with its divine power.

I am praying with you because I also have to strive evermore toward the heights, the same as you.

We, too, need much help and must not lose heart.

98

I thank you for all the love you have given me this past year.

How rich you have made me,—how much you have helped me! Thank you, and again thank you!

Together we shall walk into the new life and vow to be worthy of *Christ,* who is our helper.

*For an informative catalog of the work of Rudolf Steiner
and other anthroposophical authors please contact*

ANTHROPOSOPHIC PRESS
3390 Route 9, Hudson, New York 12534
TEL: 518-851-2054   FAX: 518-851-2047

website: www.anthropress.org